TIGHT LINES

Observations of an Outdoor Philosopher

DON MOYER

ISBN: 1452851980
ISBN-13: 9781452851983

ABOUT THE AUTHOR

Don Moyer began writing his outdoor column, *Tight Lines*, at *The Tracy Press* in 1979. As years went by he added other northern California newspapers in Ceres, Brentwood, Elk Grove, Escalon, Galt, Lathrop, Manteca, Marysville, Oakdale, Ripon, Riverbank, Turlock, and Yuba City. The column *Tight Lines* may be obtained from Don at don.moyer@gmail.com.

Also a freelance fishing writer, his work has appeared in *Angler, Flyfishing the West*, and *Sunset* magazines. Don is a native Californian and resides about 300 yards from the Stanislaus River in Ripon, California, where he and his wife, Mary, raised their 3 children.

An angler and hunter since childhood, Don has been active in fishing and hunting conservation groups for decades. A former Region Manager of California Trout and member of Trout Unlimited and the Federation of Flyfishermen, Don also served on the Board of Directors of the Tuolumne River Trust. On the hunting side of the coin, he has been a member of The Rocky Mountain Elk Foundation, Ducks Unlimited, the NRA, and the Outdoor Writers of America. Don has testified as an expert witness before the U.S. Senate and House of Representatives, both houses of the California Legislature, and numerous administrative and regulatory agencies.

When not out fishing or hunting, Don is President of Moyer Consulting, a firm specializing in fighting government red tape.

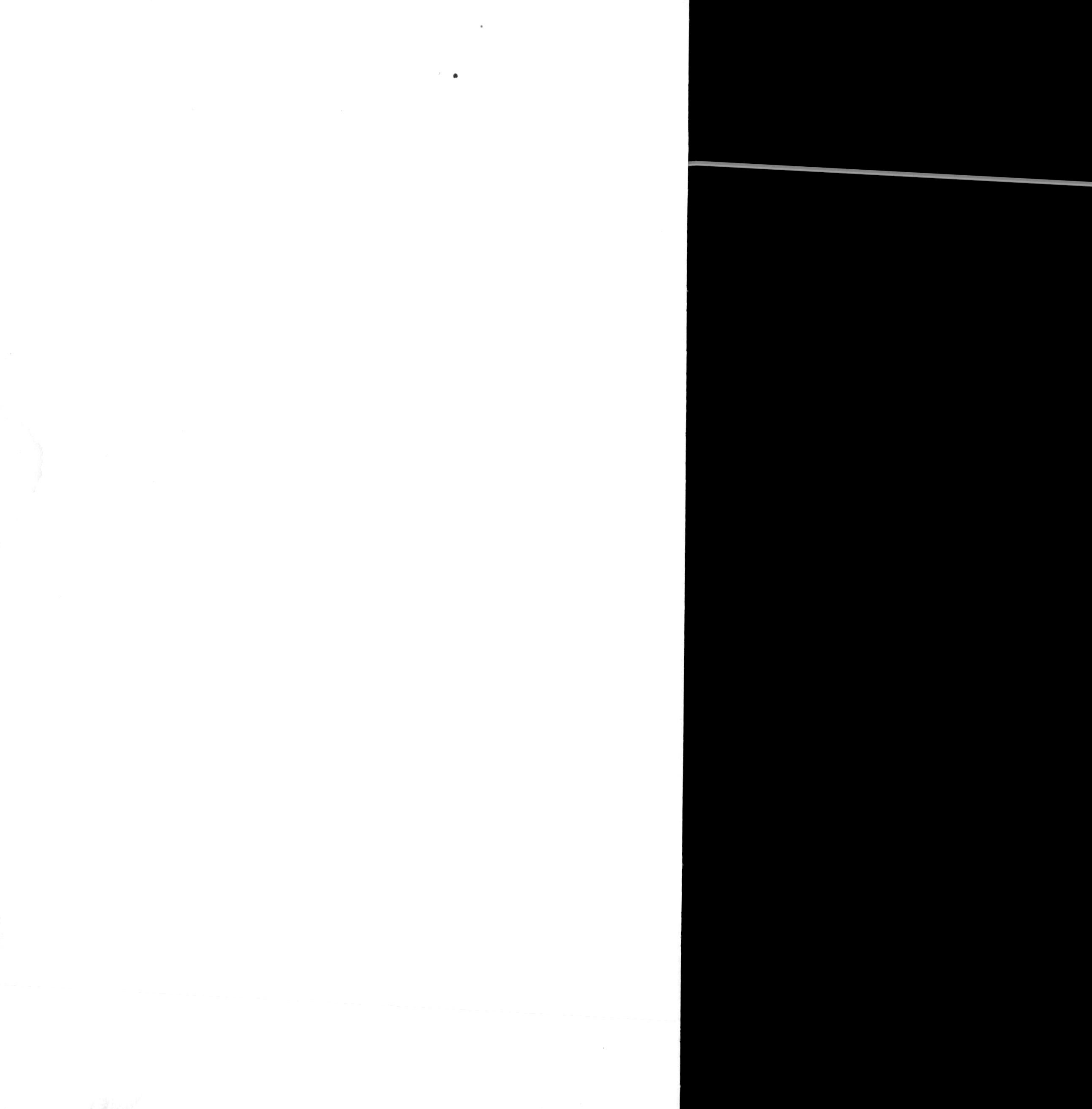

ABOUT THIS BOOK

Tight Lines: Observations of an Outdoor Philosopher is a collection of Don's most memorable columns and magazine articles over the past 30 years. They cover not only traditional fishing and hunting topics, but such diverse outdoor pursuits, as fly tying, reloading, theology, ghost towns, wilderness hot tubs, arrowhead collecting, woodcutting, conservation, guns, knives, rattlesnake wrangling, and Second Amendment rights. You may agree with him. You may think he's dead wrong. He might make you laugh, cry, or angry, but whether you agree or disagree, he'll surely make you think. *Tight Lines* is truly the observations of an outdoor philosopher.

DEDICATION

This book is dedicated to my bride of forty years, **Mary Gayle**, without whom this work would not have been possible. I thank you with all my heart.

ACKNOWLEDGEMENTS

I'd like to thank my parents, Don and Marie Moyer, who introduced me to the wonderful world of the outdoors. In addition, there are others to whom I am in debt: my wife, Mary, Mrs. Helen Fox of Ripon, who provided invaluable assistance in proof reading and editing. To my children, Julie, Melissa and Bo, who have provided me with the material for so many of my columns, thanks for letting me share my outdoor world with you. To my friends, Don McGeein, Robert Snell, Pete Simpson, and David Chezan, thanks for being my fishing partners. And finally to the newspapers who gave me my start in the outdoor column business, *The Tracy Press* and *The Manteca Bulletin*. I hope this book is worthy of all of you.

DON MOYER, May 2010

TABLE OF CONTENTS

Section One
CONSERVATION

ANGLING PARADISE LOST

September 1981

Some of my earliest and best fishing memories are of a once great fishing river, the mighty Tuolumne. I caught my first really big trout there, a rainbow just over 22 inches. I saw my first bald eagle in the Tuolumne canyon, circling higher and higher until it was just a speck that vanished over the canyon rim. I found my first rattlesnake on the Drew Ridge Trail and was held spellbound in both fear and fascination. On one trip, it rained the whole weekend, and my brother and I had a ball. Our dad found a big rock overhang and showed us how to build a fire in a pouring rain, and how to find dry wood even though it had been raining for days.

The place was called Early Intake, and it was a great place to fish for beginners and experts alike. For almost four miles the river was fairly level and averaged almost 50 yards across. The trail was a gentle one that even a first time hiker could easily walk. There were broad meadows along the way and at the trails end was a magnificent waterfall with a great swimming hole at its base. The fishing was super. Beginners like my brother and me, could hop along the boulders near the shore and catch rainbows and an occasional brown trout from 6 to 10 inches. The experts would wade out chest deep into the heavy water and be rewarded with deep-bellied browns and rainbows from 12 inches up.

Going to Early Intake was like old home week. It seemed as though every time you fished there, you ran into someone you knew. There were regulars there from Tracy, Escalon, Manteca, Modesto, Oakdale, and Stockton. I remember Frank Adams, Bill Grove, Jim Harrison, Jerry Hodges, Skip Horn, Art Kaku, Art Klugow, and Carl Upton. I'm pretty sure I recall seeing Jim Meservy, Stony Snell and Don Ringler up there too. The old pros don't fish Early Intake anymore, and I think I know why. The fishing isn't great at Early Intake anymore; it's only mediocre. The river is less than half the size it used to be. Less water means less fish, San Francisco stole our water to fill their swimming pools and water their lawns. Congressman Norm Shumway once made the observation that the Bay Area folks who oppose the filling of New Melones Reservoir on the Stanislaus River are the same folks who are taking our water from the Mokelumne River and the Tuolumne River. Right now, we've got a chance to get some of our water back from San Francisco. That water can restore the great trout fishery at Early Intake and then be used for irrigation downriver by farmers or help improve water quality in the Delta. It's a long, complicated story, but the gist of it all is that San Francisco agreed to provide minimum flows in the river which would benefit not only the fishery, but all the other downstream uses.

I need your help, all I need from you is a statement telling how good the fishing used to be. It's too late for Frank Adams, Art Klugow and Don Ringler to go back and catch the big ones at Early Intake. But it's not too late for the rest of us. Who knows? Maybe you, or your kids, or your grandkids can enjoy the kind of fishing we used to have.

On a lighter note, I'd like to thank G. I. Jones, for the memo pads depicting a guy in a business suit with his feet up on his desk, fishing rod in hand, and a hatful of flies and lures on his head. The caption most appropriately reads, "I'd rather be fishing." I guess G. I. almost split a gut laughing when I told him that wearing my fishing hat while sitting at my typewriter helps put me in the proper frame of mind to write about fishing. Thanks, G. I. that's mighty thoughtful of you. If only hope your kindness doesn't get you in trouble at Lion's Club.

⌘ ⌘ ⌘

WHO PAYS FOR CONSERVATION?

January 1982

Last week I wrote about hunting as both an effective game management tool and as an act of compassion. That got me thinking about some of the more pragmatic financial aspects of both hunting and fishing.

It's ironic to think of both money and of things that are wild and free in the same context. Have you ever heard wild geese honking in the distance and then looked up to see a flock so high you could hardly see the individual birds in the "V" formation flying south? Did you ever see spawning salmon so thick that they literally covered the bottom of a river 50 yards wide? Or did you ever watch a bald eagle fly so close overhead that you could see the individual feathers in his breast? Anyone who has ever beheld such a sight must surely be enriched because of it.

Such enthralling sights never cease making me more appreciative of nature. I sometimes think of three separate incidents which serve to remind me of the connection between the mundane financial aspects and the fleeting beauty of some of Mother Nature's finest work.

A few years ago, I was camped in the Sierra and found myself next to a friendly couple who were real hiking enthusiasts. They neither hunted nor fished, but rather carried binoculars and a camera. One afternoon, the couple came back from a hike all excited because they had seen a flock of wild turkeys as well as a dark, furry creature about the size of a large tomcat which they deduced was a pine marten.

I had run into a lady a few years before who makes an annual pilgrimage to the San Luis wildlife refuge near Los Banos to observe and photograph the herd of native Tule Elk that reside there. She also enjoys hiking and bird watching and is very concerned about the preservation of native species like the San Francisco Garter Snake, San Joaquin Kit Fox, and the Desert Pupfish. No kidding, there really are such species.

I also used to know an artist who regularly went on trips to a box canyon out in the Southern California desert to sketch the Bighorn Sheep he found there, A variety of wildlife came to water at the concrete "guzzler" placed there by the Department of Fish and Game to catch and hold water for use by desert animals. Wherever guzzlers are placed, wild creatures abound. In each of these situations, the people involved were appropriately impressed with the beauty of nature, yet at the same time, not one of them ever thought about who paid the bill so that they could enjoy such beauty, I know, here's where you think, "Hold everything! God created those critters. What's all this about paying the bill?" Here's a little food for thought.

Those impressive wild turkeys never, ever, lived in California until Fish and Game biologists brought them from the East and released them here. Tule Elk were almost extinct until a cattle baron named Henry Miller decided to preserve the last breeding pair on his ranch. Since that time, our faithful D.F.G. has watched over the elk and nurtured them until they're safe from extinction.

The magnificent wild Bighorn Sheep the artist paints were reintroduced by government game biologists after being pushed to the brink of extinction because they couldn't cope with domestic sheep for food nor tolerate the disease borne by them.

Biologists and game specialists are swell people, but do you think they work for nothing? And it's not your tax dollars paying the bill. Its anglers and hunters who've been paying the bill for all of this century. At both the state and federal levels, sportsmen (and women) have been the first groups to ever ask to be taxed so that there'd be money to help the wild creatures they love, Every time a hunter buys a gun or ammunition and every time an angler buys a fishing rod or lures, the manufacturer pays a tax to the federal government, to be used solely to benefit fish and animals.

Over and above that, angling and hunting license fees provide about 90 percent of all monies received by state fish and game departments. A year or so ago, sportsmen from all over the state, including me, lobbied the state legislature to raise our license fees so that all wild critters could benefit. Note that all wild creatures benefit, including non-game species like bald eagles, kit foxes and even garter snakes.

We all may enjoy these creatures, but it's the hunters and anglers who're paying the bill. If you really want to help those beautiful wild things, even if you don't fish or hunt, run out today and buy a hunting or fishing license. The money won't be spent on anything but fish and game. Where else can you be sure your taxes won't be frittered away on ridiculous programs?

Two months ago, I made my yearly visit to the Ducks Unlimited dinner. Anything from a three-piece business suit to an Army surplus jacket was acceptable attire. Millionaires rubbed shoulders and broke bread with farm hands. The common bond that brought such an unlikely group together was their love of free flying waterfowl. Together they raised over $75,000 in one night. All over the country, D. U. chapters raise millions of dollars to lease thousands of acres of land in Canada for nesting grounds.

The next time you see a flock of wild geese winging its way south or a 40-pound salmon leaping a waterfall on its way to spawn, thank the good Lord, because he created them, but thank your neighborhood sportsman too, because he paid the bill.

⌘ ⌘ ⌘

THE WORLD'S RAREST TROUT

February 1983

Bet you didn't know that the world's rarest trout lives right here in California and that you can probably catch one if you're crazy enough to try. The Paiute Cutthroat Trout (*Salmo Clarki Seleniris*) is so rare because it was native to only one section of one stream in the entire world. I'd say that's pretty rare. Paiutes were originally found isolated between two waterfalls on a stretch of Silver King Creek which is a tributary of the Carson River in a remote section of the Sierra Nevada Mountains.

Paiutes were transplanted above Llewellyn Falls early in the 20th century by a Basque sheepherder. Old Juan Jansaras may not have known it at the time, but his coffee can transplants probably saved the Paiute Trout from extinction. Over the years rainbows and cutthroats managed to get into the original Paiute range and destroy the pure Paiute strain by crossbreeding. Over the past 50 years the California Department of Fish and Game and U.S. Fish and Wildlife Service have been trying to eliminate the hybrid trout and restore the purple Paiutes to their original waters.

The fight to save the Paiute has been a long and difficult one, and plenty of mistakes have been made along the way. Well meaning but misguided individuals transplanted the rainbows and cutthroats above Snodgrass Falls that inadvertently endangered the Paiutes. Then the problem was compounded by aerial fish drops by DFG in the 1950s or 1960s into high country lakes that drained into the Paiute range. I guess the pilot just dropped his load of fish in the wrong lake. Matters were compounded even further by fishing by U.S. Marines out of a nearby Marine high mountain training camp. Don't get me wrong, I have the highest regard for Marines and fisheries professionals, it's just that we have made some mistakes and now we're trying to correct them so we can save this beautiful little trout.

For a few years in the early 1960s it was possible to legally fish for Paiute hybrids in the high mountain meadows of the Silver King Creek. Several buddies and I and our dads would back pack 7 or 8 miles into Silver King Valley to catch and release hundreds of rainbow/Paiute hybrids. We'd keep a few for dinner or breakfast the following day, but by removing the hybrids were actually helping the situation. The broad alpine meadows were decorated by a meandering knee-deep creek that was lined with a profusion of magnificent wildflowers. We'd dig a few wild onions along the creek and fry the Paiute hybrids in our skillet with bacon and onions. Dear Lord, my taste buds thought they had died and gone to Heaven.

Now, for the first time in 40 years, it looks as though you and I can once again catch Paiute hybrids in a setting that is about as close to Heaven as we're gonna get on this earth. The hike in isn't easy, and your muscles are going to ache some, but as you sit around the campfire watching the stars and listening to the coyotes serenade you, suddenly your aches seem to vanish and you think that it's a trip well worth the effort. If you want more information on how and where to find the incredibly beautiful Paiute Trout just drop me a line at don.moyer@gmail.com.

⌘ ⌘ ⌘

LAHONTAN CUTTHROATS

February 1983

Last week in this space I discussed the comeback of the endangered Paiute Trout. While they've still got a long way to go before large numbers of anglers will realistically be able to cast to them, a close relative of the Paiute, the Lahontan Cutthroat, has made a similar comeback and is now available for anglers to catch.

Though originally abundant enough to support a commercial fishery in Lake Tahoe on the California-Nevada border, and in Pyramid Lake in Nevada, by the end of World War II, Lahontans were practically extinct. Lahontans (*Salmo Clarki Henshawi*) were originally found only in three eastern Sierra Nevada river drainages: the Walker, Carson, and Truckee rivers.

While Paiutes are relatively small, have few or no spots, and are found in inaccessible high elevation locations, Lahontans grow to monstrous size, (world record - 41 lbs.) are heavily spotted, and are usually accessible by car. Currently you can fish for Lahontans in Pyramid Lake, Nevada, where 10 pound fish are caught every year, and in Martis Lake near Truckee, California.

One of the greatest assets, and at the same time, one of the greatest liabilities of the Lahontan Trout is that they are extremely easy to catch. Under ordinary conditions they are easily fished out, but with the use of catch and release regulations, they provide excellent sport fishing indefinitely. The use of catch and release regulations with Lahontans has been demonstrated a tremendous success at Martis Lake.

Perhaps because of their success at Martis Lake and their previous and perhaps even greater success on Hat Creek in Northern California, an unusual alliance has evolved between California's Department of Fish and Game and a citizen conservation group called California Trout. Year after year Cal Trout has asked for a catch and release fishery at Heenan Lake, located on Monitor Pass, about 10 miles southeast of Markleeville. Each year the department has expressed interest in doing such a project, but has been prevented from doing so by lack of funds, staff, and projects given higher priority.

Heenan Lake has never been open to fishing since it has been the brood stock lake from which the D.F.G. has been getting its Lahontan Cutthroat eggs for rearing and stocking in other waters. Fish in excess of 5 pounds are observed every spring at the D.F.G. egg taking station on little Heenan Creek. Last year, a breakthrough occurred which seems to have gotten the Heenan Lake fishery off dead center. The D.F.G. was able to purchase 1,600 acres of land around Heenan Lake, and the fishery experts at D.F.G. are seriously considering trying a catch and release fishery next year. In one move, the Lahontan Trout waters open to California anglers could more than double in size.

Catch and release at Martis Lake has been such a tremendous success that at times it is almost overcrowded. Opening Heenan to similar angling would help solve the problem and provide more angling opportunities for the giant Lahontans. The California Department of Fish and Game and Cal Trout should be commended for their far-sighted planning. Heenen should prove to be another fishery management success story where average anglers as well as handicapped anglers who cannot walk into the back country stand a good chance to catch and release the fish of a life time.

To D.F.G. and to Cal Trout, thank you. We anglers appreciate it.

⌘ ⌘ ⌘

RICHARD CHAMBERLAIN

August 1983

So what's such a big deal about the Tuolumne? Why's everybody getting so excited about a river? That's the part that's so fascinating, almost everybody who falls in love with the Tuolumne has a different reason. I love her because of her unmatched fishing, Richard loves her for her incredible beauty, and bird watchers find bald eagles there, while deer hunters stalk the denizens of the Jawbone Ridge deer herd.

The Tuolumne is perhaps the classic example of the concept of multiple use. There are already five dams on the river capable of storing (if you can believe this) more than the entire run-off of water in the average year.

Water from the Tuolumne irrigates over a quarter of a million acres, provides drinking water for over 2 million people and more than 2 billion kilowatt hours of electricity every year. The river provides fishing and hunting opportunities in a setting of rugged wilderness, yet, at the same time, also provides the opportunity for more urbanized pastimes like trolling for trout, house boating or waterskiing. Despite all of its development, the Tuolumne has a roadless stretch of more than 20 miles that provides a wilderness experience for those who need it.

There is a threat to the balance that makes the Tuolumne the foremost multiple use river in the world. Modesto and Turlock irrigation districts want to destroy the river by building a project that will flood half of the river that remains, and dry up the other half. Do they plan to irrigate more land to feed a starving world? No. The proposed project will provide no irrigation water at all. Do we need more flood control on the

Tuolumne? The past season was the wettest year in history, yet the Tuolumne never flooded. How about drinking water? Nope, that's not what the project is for either. What could possibly be the motive to destroy an incredible national treasure like the Tuolumne? What else but money? M.I.D. and T.I.D. already provide power to their customers at one of the cheapest rates in the entire country. They have more power than they need, and they sell the surplus to PGandE at full price. Folks in Modesto pay far less to cool their homes than you or I, yet now they want to destroy what's left of the Tuolumne so they can have even cheaper power.

The worst part of all is that not only the river itself, but almost all of the lands involved, belong to the U.S. taxpayers. Does it sound fair to you to destroy a river that belongs to 250 million of us so that 250,000 people can get free money? It sure doesn't sound fair to me.

I had never met Richard Chamberlain until last week, but it seems that he, too, has roots on the Tuolumne. He relates a delightful story of remembering looking at old pictures in the family photo album. Among them were snapshots of his grandparents in their fishing attire. He tells of going through his grandfather's fishing tackle and marveling at the old flies. Only recently, he asked his mother where his grandparents used to fish. You guessed it, the Tuolumne.

Although he's never been a fanatical trout fisher up to now, Richard expressed an interest in my offer to teach him. That is, if the river's still there for us to fish in. If you'd like to fish the Tuolumne, or have your grandchildren able to fish it, why don't you drop a quick note to the Tuolumne River Trust, Fort Mason Center, Building C, San Francisco, CA 94123. They'll tell you how to help. Who knows? If the river's still there, maybe you'll run into Richard Chamberlain out there fishing.

⌘ ⌘ ⌘

THE RETURN OF RARE WILDLIFE

November 1997

Last week, I managed to get out with my son Bo, and my friend Charlie Harris, for a little pheasant hunting. You'll notice I said hunting not shooting. One of the basic precepts of hunting is that you don't always succeed in shooting a critter. In our case, we never even saw a pheasant, but still, we were afield on a glorious sunny afternoon and enjoyed the sunshine, exercise, and camaraderie. It was a magnificent time; unless you count the short time spent wading through ankle deep chicken manure. Hoo boy! Does that stuff stink! If Charlie ever offers to take you to a secret hunting spot near a chicken farm, you may want to have made prior plans for a root canal. Just kidding, Charlie, but I'm still trying to get that smell off my boots.

I haven't seen any official figures, but it sure seems to me that the pheasant population is way down from what it used to be 20 or 30 years ago. The good news is that while pheasant populations may be down, there has been resurgence in the numbers of all sorts of other wild critters in California. Again, these observations are strictly my own, with no documentation from Fish and Game, but it seem to me that there are far greater numbers of black bear and mountain lions then there were in the fifties and sixties. In addition, there are increases in the populations of some more exotic creatures.

Several years ago, I read about a college student who was studying small fur bearers between Lake Tahoe and Susanville. As part of his research, the fellow was running a trap line to obtain specimens to study. He soon developed a problem with some sort of larger predator raiding his traps and eating the small critters trapped therein. Being a bright young grad student the guy set out to catch the malfeasor that was raiding his traps. An entire season of effort produced no results, except that the grad student was finally able to get some hair samples which the trap raider had left on a barbed wire fence. Lab analysis revealed that that the hairs were left by a wolverine! Pretty amazing, huh? Heck, I didn't even know we ever had wolverines in California.

Twice so far this year Bo and I have seen elk right here in San Joaquin County. Really, honest to goodness elk. About twenty years ago DFG biologists transplanted about 25 elk from Owens Valley up to a large park on the other side of Mount Hamilton. The elk were being held in a corral up in a remote part of the park to get them acclimated to the area prior to their release. When I hiked up to see them just before their release, I was carrying my baby daughter Julie in a backpack. Julie is a student in college now, and the elk have prospered in the past 20 years. On Memorial Day, Bo and I saw a magnificent four point bull while we were hunting wild boar. Then just a month or so ago, we were up in Corral Hollow Canyon near the Carnegie State Cycle Park when Bo, and his friend, Danny Rocha, and I spotted a herd of 15 to 20 elk that we could see right from the paved road. That was pretty cool!

While most people don't realize it, there has always been a resident population of road runners in San Joaquin County. They reside way back in the hills between Tracy and Livermore where very few people ever see them. I've mentioned before that we also have a huge and seemingly ever expanding population of wild pigs in the same area. They are expanding like wildfire and getting to be serious pests. When a herd of wild pigs comes through your ranch, the ground looks as though it has been worked over with a rototiller. The pigs wipe out crops, wildflowers, and bird eggs. They foul water supplies, cause erosion, and tear up fences. They are so prolific that there is no limit to the number of wild pigs you are allowed to shoot in a day.

I have spent my entire life enjoying the outdoors, and for my first forty years never saw an antelope in California. But within the past 10 years I've seen them on two occasions out near the Nevada border. Wild turkey were non-existent when I was a kid, yet now they have flourished and a really skilled hunter can go out and have a reasonable chance of putting a wild turkey on the table for Thanksgiving. It's not uncommon at all to find sizable flocks of wild turkey wandering down into rural barnyards and mingling with the barnyard chickens.

I always loved to watch the raptors, the birds of prey. From the little sparrow hawks all the way up to the great horned owls, and eagles, it's fascinating to watch these master hunters cruise the sky in search of their next meal. Although we always had an abundance of red tailed hawks, and there were golden eagles in the foothills, it wasn't until I was in my late 20s before I saw my first bald eagle in California. He cruised the air currents above the canyon I was fishing, and I stood transfixed in wonder, just watching until he finally cruised over the ridge out of sight. Now, bald eagles are pretty common, and you can spot them every winter along the major foothill reservoirs.

Did you ever go to the Academy of Science in San Francisco and see the stuffed California Grizzly on display? I always thought it was kind of sad that the great bear that adorns our flag was no more. Wouldn't it be magnificent if the California Grizzly were still with us? I'll let you in on a little secret, they are still with us. No jive! I know a fellow who is a licensed bear guide, and who has hunted bear in California for almost 50 years. You can tell a guy is a real bear hunter when he begins to roll up his sleeves and pant cuffs to show you his scars. Or when he takes out his glass eye. This guy knows bears like Arnold Palmer knows golf. A couple of years ago my bear guide buddy was backpacking in a really remote part of California when he was charged by a grizzly. A novice hiker might mistake a large black bear for a grizzly, but not this guy. Is it possible there are still some wild grizzlies in some really remote corner of California? I believe there are.

We have much to be grateful for in California, a great climate, fertile soil, abundant water and a wonderful array of wildlife. We should thank the good Lord for having blessed us so abundantly. We should also say thanks to our Fish and Game department and the dedicated employees who work so hard to steward these magnificent wild gifts. They are a part of our heritage and if we are careful, they can continue to be a part of our future. Hey! Get out there and enjoy that wonderful wildlife heritage of ours.

⌘ ⌘ ⌘

THE ENDANGERED RIPON BUNNY

March 2001

Some time ago, local papers have carried articles telling of the listing of the Riparian Brush Rabbit, and the Riparian Wood Rat on the list of the Federal Endangered Species Act. Most of the articles explained that both species are found only within the confines of Caswell State Park, a 258 acre wooded enclave which lies along the Stanislaus River a few miles downstream from the City of Ripon. Apparently the Riparian Brush Rabbit, also affectionately known as the Ripon Bunny, has developed an ability to climb trees when the river bottom floods. I guess that by climbing above the rising flood waters, the bunny is able to survive when other rabbits don't.

I like bunnies probably as well as anyone but, I find the press reports, if true, on both the Riparian Brush Rabbit, and the Riparian Wood Rat to be an incredible load of Hogwash. While I don't have a graduate degree in biology, I have some degree of common sense and 50 years experience in the outdoors. Does anybody really that the Ripon Bunny *only* lives within the boundaries of Caswell State Park? Believe it or not, rabbits have lots of offspring.

Did you ever hear the phrase "breed like a rabbit?" I haven't met a rabbit yet who respected property lines. Does somebody really think that the cute little bunny won't wander downstream onto the next ranch? Or upstream onto that ranch as well? Bull! I have floated every mile of the Stanislaus from Caswell downstream to its mouth at Sturgeon Bend on the San Joaquin. I have also floated every mile from Orange Blossom Bridge to Caswell. Almost every square foot of river frontage, both upstream and downstream is covered with riparian vegetation thick enough for bunnies. Yet the Ripon Bunny supposedly only lives at Caswell Park? Bullshit!

Someone in Washington, D.C., ought to have their head examined for listing a critter as endangered when it's obvious on the surface that the information given as reasons for its listing are so blatantly untrue. I'm going to peer into my crystal ball and predict the future. I predict that someday soon, some enterprising young wildlife student is going to discover that the Riparian Brush Rabbit is actually found on other properties as well!

Amazing! The Ripon Bunny lives elsewhere! Who'd a thunk it? Then of course, the poor landowners who are fortunate enough to have Ripon Bunnies on their ranches will be inundated with aspiring scientists searching for more of the endangered bunnies. Naturally, those lucky landowners will be hit with rules from Washington, D.C,. informing them that they can no longer burn the brush on their levees like they have for a hundred years. I could certainly understand how riverfront landowners would be extremely uncomfortable with the new endangered species listing.

⌘ ⌘ ⌘

URBAN WILDLIFE

June 2005

If you have lived in Ripon for at least 8 years, then you may recall the great Ripon lion scare of 1994, wherein there were mountain lion sightings along the Stanislaus River near Ripon. Although I was never fortunate enough to see any lions myself, I find it entirely possible that a stray lion and a couple of cubs could very well have worked their way down the Stanislaus River corridor as far as Ripon.

In recent years, I've seen mountain lions in Calaveras County, Tuolumne County and San Joaquin County in the foothill canyons West of Tracy. Mountain lion populations have grown astonishingly in the last 20 years. One estimate from a veteran game warden placed the existing statewide lion population at approximately eight times as many lions as we had in 1970. Quite truthfully, it wouldn't surprise me if more lions were spotted in the area.

While urban lions make the headlines and the evening news, there are a host of other wild critters that are increasingly being found in towns. Last week I was up working late at home when I heard an odd sound. At first I thought it might have been my son lifting weights in his room, but still 1:30 in the morning was a bit of a strange time to be lifting weights, so I decided to investigate. Lo and behold! My son was fast asleep in his bed.

The odd sound continued, and I decided to check out the garage along with my faithful hound, Buddy. When I opened the door, Buddy made a beeline for the corner of the garage where we feed the cats. All of a sudden, there was a terrible commotion and a large, economy sized raccoon with a dog in hot pursuit raced by me on his way out of the garage.

I wondered why the cats' food dish was always empty and yet the cats were always begging for more food. That crafty old coon had probably been helping himself to their food for some time. I have now set a cage type trap that catches critters live. We'll see if an old outdoorsman can outsmart an urban raccoon. Of course, I'd be really embarrassed if that coon outwitted me. Stay tuned for further bulletins.

Another neat example of wild critters that've chosen to live in the city recently is the immigration of Bushytailed Gray Squirrels. Ten or twelve years ago I would never see a gray squirrel in Ripon. It's my theory that they have been migrating down river at the rate of a couple miles a year. I saw bushy tails up near the Orange Blossom Bridge in the early 1980s and then at McHenry Park in the early 90s and began to spot them at Stouffer Park by the mid 90s. Last Sunday I saw one while I was driving down Fourth Street near the Community Center. My son, Donald, tells me he sees them at Ripon High now. I love to see the squirrels in town, it just makes my day to see a little reminder of God's wild creations right here in town. Go squirrels, go!

If you keep your eyes open you can see other examples of wild critters right in the city limits. Since wild animals usually tend to shy away from people, if you're gonna see them, you should keep a special eye out at night and during stormy weather when human activity is at a minimum. I have seen numerous foxes at night both at Stouffer Park and in the residential neighborhood nearby. One rainy afternoon I happened to spot a coyote trudging across the sand volleyball pits near the Rotary Gazebo. I don't know about you, but I really enjoy seeing our urban wildlife. Keep your eyes open and let me know if you see them too.

⌘ ⌘ ⌘

BACKYARD ELK

July 2005

Last week I mentioned that one of my favorite conservation groups was the Rocky Mountain Elk Foundation. One of you astute readers e-mailed me, inquiring why I support conserving critters that live 1,000 miles away. Thirty years ago I might have agreed with that position because California had almost no elk. Ironically, like the California Grizzly Bear, elk in California had once been plentiful and then pushed almost to the point of extinction.

Actually there are 3 sub-species of elk, and California is fortunate enough to have 2 of them. The largest elk are the Rocky Mountain Elk, followed in size by the Tule Elk and the Roosevelt Elk. At the beginning of the Gold Rush, the Central Valley was home to huge herds of Tule Elk; unfortunately the hordes of miners, found that they were great eating and soon the tule elk were all but gone. Only a few survived in remote ranches. The smaller Roosevelt Elk was pushed to a few isolated spots in the far reaches of northern California.

It was almost exactly 30 years ago that I saw my first Tule Elk in California. In an effort to re-establish the critters to their former home, a few Tule Elk were captured by the Fish and Game Department in the Owens Valley near the Nevada border and transplanted to a large county park in Santa Clara County. I had read in the local paper that the transplanted elk were being held in some corrals on Mount Hamilton for a few weeks to get them acclimated to our weather prior to their release. You could drive to within a mile or two of their temporary holding pens and after a short hike would be rewarded by the sight of Tule Elk about to be returned to their native range.

Thirty years later, the re-introduction has been a resounding success. The elk have adapted beautifully to their ancestral home and the original herd has thrived and grown tremendously. There are wild elk once again in California, from the Central Valley to the sea. Just last weekend, my son and I decided to go up into the hills southeast of Tracy and get in a little target practice plinking at cans on a friend's cattle ranch. We had just gotten out of the truck when I spotted a deer on the hillside, and then another, and then several more. I'll be darned if it wasn't a herd of a dozen elk! There were two large bulls and at least ten cows grazing up on the hillside. We watched them in absolute fascination until they grazed out of sight over the ridge.

The Department of Fish and Game along with conservation groups like The Elk Foundation have done a great job of providing incentives and assistance to ranchers for improving habitat and increasing the elk herds. Last year The Elk Foundation raised and spent several hundred thousand dollars exclusively for improving elk habitat in California. By piggy-backing with State and Federal grants they get more bang for their buck and invested over $600,000 in California habitat last year alone. When you or I donate money to the Rocky Mountain Elk Foundation, it helps improve habitat for a host of wildlife species. Your contributions are truly a wise investment in the future of California's wildlife.

While much of the Tule Elk habitat is on private property, the general public can see these magnificent animals fairly readily. The San Luis National Wildlife Refuge is just a few miles north of Los Banos and offers great access and viewing areas. Check their website via Google for details. If you'd like to take a beautiful week end day trip between now and May, take the Corral Hollow Exit off of I-580 just west of Tracy. Drive West on Corral Hollow Road past the Carnegie Cycle Park and up and over the pass toward Livermore, South of Livermore, turn South and head up Mines Road to the top

of Mount Hamilton. You can return to the Central Valley via Del Puerto Canyon and end up on I-5 near Patterson. This time of year it's a beautiful drive through green hills that will be covered with wildflowers in a few weeks. Drive slowly and keep your eyes open, and you may even spot an elk herd along the way. They're pretty timid and you've got to watch closely for them. If you should stop along the way for a picnic, be sure to keep your eyes peeled for sun-bathing rattlesnakes. They can give you a real surprise!
Give it a try; you'll be glad you did.

⌘ ⌘ ⌘

DOLLARS FOR WILDLIFE

April 2008

Last week I attended the local Friends of the NRA fundraising dinner in Modesto. The previous week was the Rocky Mountain Elk Foundation dinner in Ripon, and on May 2nd, it is the Safari Club dinner in Hughson. If you have never been to one of the many outdoor fund raising events of this nature, I highly recommend it. While I could be mistaken, it is my firm belief that Ducks Unlimited is the Grand Master of all charitable outdoor fund raising. They practically invented wildlife fundraising, and other conservation groups almost always copy the DU success model.

Never been to such an event? Here's how it usually works. You assemble for an evening of food and fun in a festive atmosphere at a local social hall and raise money for wildlife. Tickets to such an event will usually cost between $50 and $100 per person, and then once you arrive you can buy drink tickets for alcoholic beverages and raffle tickets in hopes of winning one of a host of really super prizes. The first time I ever went to an Elk Foundation dinner, a friend had given me a free ticket as a gift. I felt sort of guilty, so I bought a $20 packet of raffle tickets and lo and behold, I won a Winchester 30-06 rifle! I was delighted and could hardly believe my good fortune. I return year after year in hopes of winning more cool prizes.

Dinner is almost always roast beef or steak, accompanied by all the usual artery-clogging trimmings. You're not there to lose weight, so relax, enjoy yourself, and return to your diet the following day. Again, I'm pretty sure it was D.U. who pioneered the concept, but there is almost always a bevy of beautiful young women selling raffle tickets. Somehow they seem to sell more tickets than a bunch of ugly guys. Don't get the impression that these dinners are some kind of wild stag party because nothing could be further from the truth. Outdoor fundraisers are truly a family oriented event. You'll see husbands and wives, as well as boys and girls too. Most years, I take my son, daughters, or sons-in-law along to join in the festivities.

Once you have a bunch of raffle tickets you then have to decide which raffle item you want to try for since there are actually many individual raffles going on all at once. For example, there might be a raffle for a 7mm Remington Magnum suitable for elk or bear, another raffle for a Henry Youth Model 22, one for a gun safe, or a spotting scope, or a guided safari to Africa or Alaska. You put your raffle tickets in the bucket of the prize you most want to win. If you already have a 7mm Magnum, you may put all your tickets in the bucket to try to win a Savage shotgun or a Colt 45.

One year my son was determined that he was going to win a Colt 45, and thus we put all of our tickets in the Colt bucket and not the bucket for duck decoys. Oddly enough, you seem to get luckier as you purchase more and more tickets. Darned if we didn't win a colt 45 for my son! He was delighted and so was I. Of course, it would probably have been cheaper to just buy the gun at the local gun shop, but it's not nearly as much fun.

No, you aren't going to win, every time, but that's not the point. You're there to raise money to help pay for habitat, and wildlife easements, and even the salaries of the fish and game professionals who manage our resources for us. You buy critical migration routes, and desert water guzzlers that keep the wild game alive and prospering. If you haven't been to one of the many outdoor wildlife fundraisers, by all means get out there and do so. The critters need our help!

⌘ ⌘ ⌘

Section Two
EXPLORING AND EDUCATION

DESERT CRITTERS

September 2009

My wife thinks I'm crazy, but in addition to mountains and oceans, I love deserts. I love the wide empty spaces where there are no humans for as far as you can see. I love the singing of coyotes and the smell of sage and the desert sunsets. I love the weird critters that have adapted to desert life, and I love the freedom to be able to shoot a rifle without bothering a single human being. I love the Mojave Desert of southern California, the Forty Mile Desert of Nevada, and the Sonoran Desert of Arizona. Heck, I even love the San Joaquin Desert of the Great Central Valley. Desert? In the Central Valley?

Ironically, before the introduction of dams and irrigation, the Central Valley was a desert most of the year except when inundated by the annual springtime floods. With the advent of major dams on the rivers, the yearly floods became less and less frequent, and millions of acres of land were converted from desert to bountiful farms. Tulare Lake, north of Bakersfield, was roughly the size of Lake Tahoe and now it's gone. Owens Lake, east of the Sierras, was so big it supported paddle-wheel steamboats that crossed the lake daily delivering supplies to the mines on the other side. It's gone too. If you ask enough old timers, some of them can recall when local kids caught horned toads for pets and you had to watch for a rattler in the hay stacks. Even in the 1960s before completion of the California Aqueduct, there were vast reaches of alkali flats along the route of what is now I-5.

Believe it or not, there are still a few remnants of the San Joaquin Desert and they teem with critters that don't exist except in the desert. Last weekend, a buddy, Hercules, and I were up in one of the Coast Range canyons that connect to the valley when we spotted a looked like a scrawny pheasant standing near the road. Herc had never seen one before, and I don't think he believed me when I told him it was a roadrunner. We stopped the truck about 30 feet from the bird and walked toward it, and sure enough, it ran out of sight. The hills to our west have become a de facto refuge for the desert critters that formerly resided in the San Joaquin Desert. In addition to roadrunners, there are horned toads, rattlesnakes, king snakes, jack rabbits, cottontails, brush rabbits, scorpions, mountain lions, bobcats, deer, elk, golden eagles, and shrikes. I've probably overlooked a few, but I think you get the idea. Heck, there are even coyotes that try to make a meal out of the roadrunners.

If you'd like to get a little sample of the desert environment of those hills there are still some opportunities to do so. Several public roads cross the hills and provide opportunities for wildlife viewing. Carnegie State Vehicular Recreation Area is on Corral Hollow Road southwest of Tracy. It has 1,500 acres and is open to camping with 23 spaces available on a first come, first served basis. Frank Raines Park is on Del Puerto Canyon Road west of Patterson and also has public access and campsites. At the moment Frank Raines Park is closed due to the high fire danger, so check it out on Google before you go. A little further south, San Luis Reservoir State Recreation Area on Pacheco Pass has lots of campsites, boating and great fishing. It's probably at San Luis that you'll stand the best chance of seeing both Tule Elk and wild hogs.

Right now, the hills are hot and dry and the critters mostly come out at night. In fact, as teenagers we used to ride the paved roads at night to find the rattlers that crawl out on the asphalt to get warm. Interestingly, now is just about the beginning of the annual tarantula migration. Male tarantulas are on the move, seeking females for breeding season.

If you're driving the coast range hills at dusk, be on the look-out for the tarantulas. If I spot a tarantula, I usually stop and shoo them across the road with a piece of cardboard so it won't get squished. They also make great pets and can live for years in a home terrarium, although now it's easier to just buy them on the internet. No kidding, Tarantulas.com will guarantee live delivery of tarantulas to your door. Leave the wild ones out there in the wild.

There you have it, desert critters right in your backyard. Who'd a thunk it? All you have to do is get out there and introduce yourself to them!

⌘ ⌘ ⌘

WILD TROUT, NATIVE TROUT

July 1983

I have long had a love affair with brook trout; it sounds a little kinky I'll confess, but I just can't help it. I've been fishing for brookies for so long now that I honestly can't remember not having fished for them. Searching back as far in my memory as possible, I do recall an incident that took place when I was about 10 or 12 years old. My family and I had been camped, as usual in Hermit Valley near the top of Ebbetts Pass. I had wandered up one of the side creeks and caught about a dozen fat little brookies and was feeling pretty proud. I stopped along the way to show off my catch, even though I was a couple fish shy of the 15 fish limit.

One fellow got all excited when he saw my fish. "Hey, dear," he yelled to his wife, "Come over here and see the native trout this young fellow's got!" I really didn't know what all the excitement was about. Naturally, I wanted folks to notice my fish, but after all, they weren't really monsters. At the time I figured that "native" must be something pretty special. Over the years, I began to notice other anglers referring to native trout with a degree of reverence. I also began to hear people talk about wild trout in similar sorts of endearing terms.

People often used the terms "native" and "wild" interchangeably, usually contrasting them with hatchery raised trout. Although I was certain of it at the time (I'm far less certain now), hatchery trout were vastly inferior to wild and/or native fish. Because they were all the same size and shape, and when released, hatchery trout all looked pretty much alike. They were called such derisive names as "cookie cutter trout," or "G.I. Trout," or one of my favorites, "Liver Stuffed

Guppies Wrapped in Rainbow Skins." Whatever these wild or native critters were, they sure had to be better than the hatchery variety. After a couple of decades, I've finally figured out what wild and native mean. Unfortunately, what the words really mean isn't what most folks think. It's pretty simple really, avoids a lot of confusion, and impresses your friends too. A trout is native when it's found in the original waters that were historically home to that species. In the case of a brook trout, their original range was only on the Atlantic Coast from about Virginia northward into Canada. Thus, if you catch a brookie in California, there's no way it could be considered native, in New York, yes, in California, no way. If you hear someone call a brookie a "native," you can be pretty sure he's a transplanted Yankee.

Brown Trout, otherwise called the German Brown, Loch Leven, or even the Von Behr Trout, were imported from Europe and aren't native anywhere in America. Rainbows were originally found only on the Pacific Coast, while cutthroats were native to the Rocky Mountains and the West. Goldens were native only to California's Kern River watershed. Accordingly, California can legitimately claim 3 kinds of "native" trout: rainbows, cutthroats and goldens. "Wild," on the other hand, means a trout that was born and raised solely by Mother Nature with no help from the local hatchery. I still love to fish for brookies, no matter what name they're called by. Almost all brook trout in California are several generations removed from a hatchery. They are aggressive when it comes to smashing a fly, lure, or bait. They are one of the tastiest fish that swims, and they are incredibly beautiful. To top it all off, they are almost always found in crystal clear mountain streams, truly earning their Latin name *Savalinius Fontinalis*, or Little Trout of the Springs.

⌘ ⌘ ⌘

GAMEFISH PETS

I guess the practice of having animals as pets dates back as far as the human race itself. Archeology experts have found mummified cats in ancient Egyptian tombs that are thousands of years old. In modern times researchers have confirmed what most of us know intuitively, that keeping pets is good for us humans too. Over the years some of my best friends have been animals. As a general rule, wild animals don't make good pets.

Several years ago, my son and I helped rescue a batch of coyote puppies whose mother had dug her den in an orchard that was flood irrigated. Sure enough, at irrigation time the den flooded and an entire litter of newborn coyote pups had to swim for their lives. We were able to rescue several of the cute little guys and kept them in a warm box indoors and hand fed them with a medicine dropper. While it was very tempting to maybe keep one of the little critters as a pet, common sense finally prevailed, and I called my local game warden who found them a home at a wildlife shelter that eventually released them back into the wild.

While most wild critters do not adapt well as pets, warm water gamefish are a notable exception. Largemouth Bass, Smallmouth, Crappie, Bluegills and Sunfish all make fine aquarium pets. For several years I had a pet bass, whose name was Sam. Every week I'd take my live minnow bucket to the local bait shop and get a dozen minnows to feed Sam. Just before dumping the minnows into the aquarium, I'd tap on the glass with my fingernail. Pretty soon, Sam figured out that the finger tapping was his dinner bell and he'd get all excited and race around the tank in anticipation. It was sort of like the "Hungry Dog Dance" my dogs do every night at dinner time. If you'd tap on the glass and stick your finger in the tank, old Sam would figure you were a minnow and would bite your finger. I almost had several guests convinced that Sam was a man-eating bass. Over the years, I've had pet Crappie, Bluegills and Smallmouth as pets, and they all worked out fine. Because they are warm water fish, they prefer water at pretty much the same temperature as your normal household. They aren't fussy eaters and will eat minnows, table scraps, and, yes, there is even a Purina Fish Chow. Crappie is especially beautiful fish and will live in a home aquarium for years. Trout prefer colder waters and don't adapt as well to aquarium life. I've got to throw in a legal disclaimer at this point. It is illegal to catch a California gamefish and transport it out of its home water alive. There have been too many examples of how well meaning folks have transplanted fish into different waters and really screwed things up.

If you want to keep a gamefish as a pet, don't just catch a bass or crappie and bring it home in an ice chest. So how do you get a legal game fish as a pet? You buy one from a private fish breeder, who is licensed by the state. Go to the Department of Fish and Game website and click on their aquaculture link for a list of licensed fish breeders. Once you've got your legal gamefish you care for them just you would any aquarium fish. They are lots of fun and make great pets. You can even convince your friends you've got a man-eating bass.

⌘ ⌘ ⌘

BLUE SKY CLASSROOMS

October 1987

It seems as though the public schools get a lot of criticism these days, but then I'd be willing to bet that people have been complaining about schools as long as schools have existed. Certainly, some of the criticism of schools is warranted and schools could use improvement. There is, however, a good argument to be made that that we are asking our schools and their administrators and teachers to teach things that we, as parents, should be teaching to our children ourselves. Quite honestly, I'm not qualified to teach my children chemistry, music, or computer science. By the same token I know of no one more qualified to teach my kids the values, ethics and morals that I consider important.

You might wonder what the above has to do with the outdoors, and the answer is one of those philosophical answers like "everything" or "nothing at all." When I was learning to fish from my dad, I didn't realize that what I was learning was far more than simply how to bait a hook, cast a fly, or play a fish. Of course, the empirical "how to" information was the obvious part that I was learning, and my immediate goal was to be able to put lots of fish in the creel.

Subtly, however, Dad was also teaching us to enjoy the columbines, shooting stars, and other wildflowers along the stream, as well as the brilliance of sunlight striking dew drops in a spider's web. Dad enforced a rule that his father had taught him. We always took a rest after lunch and sat back on a sand bar or meadow or even a midstream boulder to watch a red-tailed hawk drift overhead or laugh at the squirrels as they scampered through the limbs above. We marveled at the construction skills of the laborers who had built rock support walls for a road on the side of a sheer canyon. When I first heard about a bird called the dipper or water ouzel, I swore it had to be some kind of joke like hunting snipes with a burlap bag. But during our afternoon breaks, I learned that there really is a bird that flies down into the water and walks along the stream bottom.

I suppose there is a sort of natural evolution that outdoor addicts progress through. It used to be very important that I return home from my fishing trips with a limit of fish. I guess it was some sort of proof that I really was a mighty angler. The same sort of "dead meat" philosophy pervaded my hunting efforts also, and for a time, I measured my success in hunting by how many dead critters I brought home. Slowly, however, that philosophy changed. I didn't realize it at the time, but through example, Dad was molding my progression as an outdoorsman. Instead of bringing home 30 fish and putting half of them in the freezer, Dad would say that he really wasn't too keen on eating frozen fish and would suggest we bring home only a dozen and release the other fish unharmed.

The emphasis in my outdoor education began to shift from how to properly cast a fly to topics such as why I should use a fly that imitates a stone fly in rocky, tumbling water or a fly that imitates a grasshopper in a grassy meadow stream. Eventually, we began to discuss the ecology of a trout stream and how everything was inextricably tied to everything else. I began to ask questions and seek the answers in books. Entomology books taught me the answers to my questions about stream insects, and soon I turned to books on trees to identify the tree that had bark that smelled like vanilla. Then there were books on flowers, weather, geology and natural history.

My trips afield were history lessons from old mining ruins and archeology lessons from arrowheads and old Indian camp sites. I learned geology by dragging home some fascinating rocks instead of dead fish. Astronomy and navigation were learned from observing the night sky around the evening campfire. And when man began to put artificial satellites into the sky, I began to understand about the physics of it all. Lessons in geography and political science evolved from questions such as "Who are these Soviets who put up the Sputnik satellite?" "Why did they put it into orbit?" Or, "Why we Americans are trying so hard to catch up?"

Such information wouldn't really help me in the spelling bee at school or in working out an algebra problem, but what the "blue sky" classrooms taught me was far more important than memorizing formulas. I learned that knowledge was fascinating, fun and even valuable, just for its own sake. I learned to love learning and learned values that aren't taught in textbooks. I learned to love blue skies, clear streams, and green forests and the creatures that live in them.

While I was in school, I learned skills that are necessary to survive in today's world, but in my blue sky classrooms I learned values from my parents, the values that make the human race different from all the other creatures on Earth. I doubt if any other creatures on this planet enjoy a sunset and wonder who might have made it and why.

The next time you get a chance, take your kids, or your grandchildren, outdoors and share with them the lessons and values that you think are important ones. Use the blue sky class rooms to teach our children the kinds of things that our school system can't teach and shouldn't teach. The Good Lord gave us some magnificent classrooms to teach in, if only we'll use them.

⌘ ⌘ ⌘

TROUT FISHING GRAND SLAM

March 1990

If you are a baseball fan, you know that a Grand Slam is when the bases are loaded and you hit a Home Run that scores 4 runs. It's sort of like hitting a hole in one in golf, really rare and really cool. Hunters too, have their own Grand Slam, which is getting one each of the four kinds of wild sheep. Some fanatics have spent their entire adult life searching all over the world, trying to get a Desert Sheep, Stone Sheep, Dall Sheep, and Marco Polo Sheep. Again, it's very rare and extremely difficult. Trout fishers also have a Grand Slam they can seek. The good news is that you don't have to be rich and travel the world in search of the four primary species of trout. You can find Rainbows, Brookies, Browns, and Cutthroats all without leaving California. In addition, we also have some pretty rare trout like Goldens, Paiutes, Mackinaws, and, depending upon who you believe, we may even have Redband Trout in California.

As you might guess, Raindows are the most plentiful trout in our fair state. Rainbow Trout, (*Salmo Iridis*) are native to California and fond of faster streams and colder lakes. They are fairly easy to raise in hatcheries and hence the most frequently planted trout released by the Department of Fish and Game. They have the distinctive reddish rainbow coloration and can grow quite large, exceeding 5 pounds in streams and reaching over 20 pounds in lakes. For most anglers rainbows are the bread and butter of trout fishing and sort of the standard against which all other trout are compared.

Brown Trout (*Salmo Trutta*) are native to Europe and were transplanted to California from a lake in Scotland (Loch

Leven) over 100 years ago. They have adapted extremely well to California waters and can tolerate slower and warmer waters than rainbows. Brownies have mostly brown spots (hence their name) and a few red spots and can grow even larger than rainbows. While all trout are predators, browns are more efficient predators and can take over a stream by eating the young of other species. Huge browns from high mountain lakes have exceeded 30 pounds. They are more wary than rainbows and harder to catch.

Brook Trout (*Savalinius Fontanalis*) were native to the eastern United States. They were transplanted here to California in the late 1890s and live up to their name by inhabiting smaller brooks and streams that have colder waters. Brookies don't usually grow as large as rainbows and browns in part because of their preference for colder waters which produce less food. They feed very aggressively and are easy to catch.

I love to fish a remote brookie stream where you can catch and release dozens of the fiesty critters. It's a great experience for a beginning angler. Brook Trout breed prolifically and can get over crowded in their home waters. Anglers catching and eating a batch of brookies can actually have a beneficial effect on their populations and allow the remaining fish to grow larger. Brooks have bright pink meat and are in my estimation the tastiest trout of all. Because of their tendency to over populate you don't have to feel guilty when you eat a batch of Brook Trout.

Cutthroat Trout, (*Salmo Clarki*) are also native to California and have a distinctive bright red band of color right behind their gills that makes them look as though they've had their throats cut and gives them their name. They are easy to catch and don't respond well to heavy fishing pressure and, as a result, are now found only in remote waters.

Cutthroat historically grew quite large and exceeded 30 pounds in Lake Tahoe and Pyramid Lake. There was even a commercial fishery in those lakes before 1900 that almost wiped out the species. They are an ideal trout for a catch-and-release fishery because they grow quite large if you keep putting them back. They can offer an average angler the chance to catch a large trout. You can take your picture with cutthroats and, as long as you keep releasing them; they will be dumb enough to be caught again tomorrow.

Here you have it: Trout Fishing's Grand Slam, consisting of rainbows, browns, brooks, and cutthroat. You don't have to be a millionaire and travel the world because you can find all four species right here in California. In fact, if you read next week's column, I'll even tell you where you can catch your very own grand slam in one stream in a single day. No kidding, you really can. Who knows? If you're interested, we can even delve into where to find the rare trouts.

⌘ ⌘ ⌘

MAMMOTH GRAND SLAM

April 1990

A couple of weeks ago I mentioned that a Trout Fishing Grand Slam consisted of catching one or more of each of the following four trout species: Rainbow Trout, Brown Trout, Brook Trout, and Cutthroat Trout. While sheep hunters have to literally spend a fortune traveling the world to hunt a sheep Grand Slam, we trout fanatics are much luckier because we can pursue our Holy Grail without ever leaving California. To top it all off, we can do so in comfort and style.

The town of Mammoth Lakes, California, is located on the eastern side of the Sierra Nevada on Highway 395. For those of us here in the San Joaquin Valley, it is a drive of several hours over the Sierra via either Tioga Pass in Yosemite Park, or via Sonora Pass just to the north. Once over the pass, turn right when you get to Highway 395 and proceed to Mammoth Lakes. I fell in love with Mammoth the first time I went there and find more to love about the place every time I return. Mammoth Lakes is an upscale Ski Resort community that provides the closest good skiing to the Los Angeles area. Like most ski resorts, it bustles with quaint restaurants and ski shops all sorts of other places to spend your money.

Also like most ski resorts, the place is vastly different in the summer off-season. The skiers are gone, the crowds are gone and you can rent a place to stay for a really decent rate. Best of all the summer trout fishing is super. There are hosts of sporting goods stores that cater to skiers in winter and anglers, bikers and hikers in the summer. Actually, the entire region is an angler's dream. There are lakes with monster trout longer than your leg, and streams choked with brookies eager to nail your fly. The whole area is a geological anomaly with volcanic activity and hot springs almost everywhere. You and your partner can soak in the romantic solitude of a volcanic hot tub with the local coyotes serenading in the background.

As inviting as the hot tubs and the gourmet restaurants are, the real reason I go is to catch my grand slam of wild trout. Like everything else in the Mammoth area, even the fishing is unlike any fishing you'll find you'll find anywhere on earth. No kidding, anywhere else, you have to backpack into the wilderness and arrive at the stream hot, sweaty, and smelling like a pack mule. At Mammoth, you take a leisurely drive to the Mammoth Mountain Ski Resort, park your car, and board a transit bus for some of the most civilized angling on earth. You ride the bus down to Red's Meadow in Devil's Postpile National Monument. You step off the bus at any one of the numerous bus stops and fish until you get tired of catching wild rainbows, browns, brooks and cutthroats. Then you get back on the bus and return to another night of quiche cuisine and coyote serenades.

I've got to give you fair warning though, the Mammoth Lakes experience is addicting. There's something for everyone, from small children to senior citizens. While I dearly love traditional wilderness fishing, the Mammoth experience could really spoil you. Give it a try and let me know what you think.

⌘ ⌘ ⌘

California Golden Poppy

WILDFLOWER EXTRAVAGANZA

March 1997

One of the best items an outdoor enthusiast can carry is one or more of the guidebooks on flowers, trees, rocks birds, or mammals that inhabit the area. I often carry one of the handy field guides in my fishing vest, or backpack. Perhaps the most dog-eared of my field guides in the one on California wildflowers.

For the next month or two, California's wildflowers will be putting on a magnificent show for all of us to enjoy. The price of admission is a tankful of gas and some wear and tear on your boots. While the high Sierra gets all the attention of trout fishers, skiers, and hunters, the most prolific wildflowers are actually a little lower down the mountain. I especially enjoy the profusion and variety of the wildflowers in the foothills at about the 1,500 foot to 2,500 foot elevation level. Living here in the Central Valley we are blessed with great wildflower viewing both in the coastal hills to our west and in the Sierra foothills to the east of us.

We have so many varieties of wildflowers in California that there's something for every taste. As a child, I remember driving over the Altamont Pass and marveling at the profusion of California golden poppies. You probably know that they are our official state flower and they were mentioned by John Muir, and almost every other early California explorer who kept a journal.

But did you know that the beautiful blue brodea have an edible bulb below the ground and were a staple food of most California Indian tribes? Of course, the flaming red Indian paintbrush weren't really red because the Indians painted with them, but it made a great story to get children interested in nature. When I picked lupines to take home to my Mom, I learned that wildflowers don't last long when you pick them. Pretty soon, I learned that wildflowers are best enjoyed when you just view them in place, where God put them.

The exception to the rule that you can't take wildflowers home with you is, of course, photography. Even an amateur photographer can often take some stunning wildflower pictures. Sure, you can take some pretty shots with your cell phone camera, but to really capture the amazing colors and variety of wildflowers, you need a real honest to goodness camera. Whether you've got a fancy new digital camera, a somewhat outdated Nikon that uses film, or even an antique Kodak from the 1950s, you ought to be able to get some great wildflower shots in the next month or two. If you get a set of close-up lenses to take pictures from 3 inches away, so much the better.

Where to go to see great wildflowers? Try one of these two suggestions:

- The Coastal Range, west of the valley, or
- The Sierra foothills, east of the valley.

Both areas make a great day trip. You can pack a picnic lunch, leave home after breakfast, and be back home by dinner. It's a great way to spend a Saturday with your spouse and kids.

My recommendation for the Coastal hills trip is to drive west of Tracy on Eleventh Street and take Corral Hollow Road South bound. Follow Corral Hollow up and over I-580 and up into the hills past Carnegie Park. Take your time as you drive and enjoy the scenery. That's why you're there. Proceed over the pass into Alameda County and turn left on Mines Road. Follow Mines Road as it winds up the mountain in a southerly direction until you get to the top where it intersects with Mount Hamilton Road. You can go west a short way to the observatory at the top of Mount Hamilton and have a picnic lunch there, or you can turn east on Mount Hamilton Road and follow it down Ospital Canyon past Frank Raines County Park in Stanislaus County. You'll come out on I-5 at the bottom of the canyon. It will take you almost all day, but it's a great trip.

If you'd rather see the Sierra foothills, drive South on Highway 99 to Merced and take Highway 140 up the Merced River Canyon to Yosemite National Park. You can have your picnic lunch along the Merced River or drive into the Park and eat like royalty at the Ahwanee Hotel. Cheap and simple, or expensive and fancy, whatever suits your pocketbook.

If you're in pretty good physical condition, you might want to stop about 10 miles east of the park boundary at Savage's Trading Post where the South Fork of the Merced joins the main river. The South Fork Trail is arguably the best wildflower hike in the world. No jive! In March and April the wildflowers along that stretch of trail are unsurpassed anywhere on earth. Watch your step because the trail drops off very steeply to the South Fork. After a couple miles or so, the trail flattens out and becomes less steep. Expect to see poppies, lupine, brodea, shooting stars, Indian paintbrush, and a host of others in the most impressive display of wildflowers you've ever seen. You can also explore the old mining ruins along the South Fork and wonder at the ingenuity of our forefathers.

On either the coastal day trip or the Sierra Foothill one, be sure to take your camera because you're gonna see some breathtaking wildflowers. Bringing your camera will enable you to capture these beautiful inhabitants of our outdoors and bring them home to enjoy for the rest of your life. Its great fun, good exercise, and another excuse to get out there and enjoy our amazing state.

⌘ ⌘ ⌘

Watch Where You Walk!

RATTLESNAKE SEASON

May 1998

Every year about this time, or so the poets would have us believe, a young man's fancy turns to love. Perhaps that's true for young men, but this is the time of year when my thoughts turn to catching rattlesnakes. Some folks think that my hobby of catching live rattlers is a little weird, and who knows? Maybe they're right. You've got to admit, though, catching rattlers is exciting. This is the time when the snakes are just coming out of hibernation, and the hills are green and studded with beautiful flowers. Some guys will resort to any excuse to get outdoors.

Last weekend my snake catching partner, Don McGeein, my 11 year old son Bo, and I sallied forth to try our luck. Don is a darned good amateur taxidermist and does a great job mounting some of the snakes we catch. Rattlers also make great hatbands and belts. Our goal this weekend, though, was to obtain some rattlers for Bo's Boy Scout patrol. Let's face it: Troop 414's Sidewinder Patrol would not be complete without a real honest-to-goodness rattlesnake skin for the Patrol Banner.

Over the years Don McGeein and I have worked out a pretty good system for catching the rattlers and putting them into the sack. We have snake proof leggings that reach up to our knees, and four foot long snake grabbers that we grab the little beggars with. When one of us grabs a snake the other guy holds open a cloth drawstring bag while the snake is carefully lowered into the sack. Young Bo has accompanied us for several years and has shot some rattlers with his 22, but until last weekend he'd never actually picked one up with the grabbers and bagged him. Last Saturday, we hadn't been out too long before Don spotted a nice rattler sunning himself on a pile of logs. Bo handled the snake quite well and lowered him into the bag which I was holding open as old Don took pictures for the historic occasion. After we had properly gassed the snake with ether, we measured him at a respectable 42 inches including his 10 rattles.

Hopefully, you're not as crazy as I am, and don't go out searching for rattlers. But the fact of the matter is, if you spend much time outdoors you might run across a rattler. More often than not, most rattlers are not very aggressive and will avoid you if they can. If you should find a rattler, your best course of action is to simply back away and leave it alone. Chances are, if you leave the snake alone, it will leave you alone. In fact, oftentimes, it will go the other way even when you've provoked it.

Your best defense is really quite simple: "Watch Where You Walk." It's not very exotic, but all you have to do is get into the habit of looking down every few seconds. That way, you know where you're going to be putting your feet, and you'll save yourself a lot of trouble. Not only will you be able to avoid snakes, but you will reduce your chance of falling on a loose rock and maybe twisting an ankle or breaking a leg. Don't step over logs or rocks either; step on top of the log or rock. The reason for this is simple: rattlesnakes like to hide under logs and rocks.

Another wise idea to consider if you spend much time afield is to get one of the modern snake bite kits called "The Extractor." They are ten times more effective than the old suction cup type, and are readily available from your local pharmacy at about $15.00.

It's cheap insurance and great peace of mind. Remember, the outdoors can be an amazing amount of fun, and if you watch where you walk, it will most likely stay fun. Remember: "Watch Where You Walk."

⌘ ⌘ ⌘

THE JEEP

May 2002

Our 1946 Jeep was our passport to excitement. We explored the back country of the Sierra Nevada Mountains on our way to camping, endless trout fishing and exploration of desert ghost towns. Although our jeep took our family to magical places, it gave us cause for concern too. Once, when driving down a steep mountain pass, the steering wheel came off, and we had to jury-rig the jeep with a pipe wrench and bailing wire and steer it like a tiller. Despite it all, our beloved jeep always got us there and back. That jeep was like one of the family!

Like a family member, the jeep had multiple flaws that we learned to live with. It had no heater, and in winter you had to bundle up like an Eskimo just to survive a ride in it. Except for the driver, everyone else bundled up in sleeping bags for a winter drive and just stuck our heads out of the sleeping bags. There were no turn signals, so you stuck your arm out the side and used arm signals to turn. Somehow, some kid dropped a length of string into the gas tank and periodically the string would get sucked into the fuel line and block it completely. As you were driving along, you never knew if the jeep was going to sputter to a sudden stop. No problem, you just got out and vigorously rocked the jeep up and down by hand until the string floated loose, and you could continue on your way.

The old jeep had an intermittent electrical short of some sort that regularly drained the battery. You could rely on one thing for sure, when you really needed the jeep to start, the battery was dead. Again, as Arnold would say, "No Problemo." You parked on an incline whenever possible, rolled down the hill or driveway a little way and popped the clutch to start. That worked once in a while, but there are very few hills in the central valley, and not much slope in a supermarket parking lot. We had a solution for that too. Every time you went for a ride, you picked up as many of your buddies as possible and everyone would push as fast as he could so you could pop the clutch and start it. Then you drove around the block and slowed down so that the stragglers could jump on the moving jeep.

A trip in the jeep was almost always an adventure. On the old immigrant road between Hermit Valley on Highway 4 and Hope Valley on Highway 88 we hit a rock especially hard and knocked a hole in the oil pan. Vehicles don't go far with a hole in the oil pan. As usual, we improvised, and carved a wooden plug to drive into the hole.

We regularly had extra oil cans, and when we refilled the oil, the wooden plug absorbed some of it and swelled until the oil leak stopped almost completely and we were able to limp back to civilization. We had a similar event with the radiator petcock, the little faucet with which you drain your radiator. Slamming it with a rock will break off the petcock every time. Sure enough, the water drains right out and your vehicle comes to a sudden stop. Once again the old wooden plug, carved to fit will make a jury-rigged repair, and you can refill your radiator and limp home again. Sometimes refilling the radiator in the desert can be a challenge, but if you put you mind to it, you'll find a way.

Driving the old jeep was a challenge, and you had to be careful not to flip it over. It sat very high up off the road and had a short wheel base, which was great for maneuvering through tight spots, but if you took a corner too fast, the jeep would flip over and spill both passenger and contents. Usually everybody dusted themselves off and we flipped the jeep right side up and continued on our way. You also had to be careful of side hill roll-overs, because if you rolled it down the side of a mountain, that was much more serious.

Why would anyone want to have or even ride in, such a traveling death trap? It's sort of like the answer to "Why Climb a Mountain?" Because it's there. Sure, it's a lot more comfortable traveling across the desert in your air conditioned truck, with the cruise control set at 78 miles an hour. You can listen to your favorite music in stereo, and take care of business on your cell phone. But somehow, I think I saw more wildlife and explored more old overgrown logging roads with the beat up old jeep. Heck, today you're afraid you might scratch your high gloss paint or get a ding in the chrome bumper. I saw an old original jeep in a ranch barnyard awhile back. It's in parts, but it looks like most of the major stuff is there. I wonder if my son and I could put the old gal back together. Now, if I can just convince my wife, I might even have it ready by deer season.

⌘ ⌘ ⌘

Yosemite in Spring

YOSEMITE IN SPRINGTIME

March 2003

It's ironic how we tend to overlook those things closest to home. I once spent an entire summer in Washington, D.C., and never stopped to see the Smithsonian Institution, Jefferson Memorial or Arlington Cemetery. I rode past Lincoln Memorial and the Washington Monument every day on the way to work and never once stopped there either.

People come from all over the world to visit California and make special trips to see Yosemite National Valley, yet I never saw Yosemite Valley until I was a high school senior. The only reason I went that time was to impress my girlfriend with how great my new sports car handled on mountain roads. I was more impressed with the beauty of Yosemite than I was with the young lady. A lot of cars and girls have come and gone since then but I'm still awed by the majesty of Yosemite. I avoid Yosemite Valley in mid-summer because I dislike the crowds of people, bus exhaust fumes, barking dogs and discarded candy wrappers. All the rest of the year, however, Yosemite Valley is magnificent. Of course, the back country of the park is always better than the crowds of the valley.

Yosemite is beautiful in winter when it's all covered with snow and the waterfalls are bedecked with icicles shimmering in the winter sun. In fall, the color of the turning leaves is breathtaking, and I marvel at the sight of waterfalls that fall off a cliff and vanish because they dissipate into a fine mist and evaporate before they reach the bottom.

Of all the times to visit Yosemite, the most spectacular of all is right now. Rain and melting snow have turned every stream into a roaring torrent. The valley literally shakes from the vibrations of all the cascades, the peaks are covered in white, while the meadows below have turned into a squishy sea of new grown grass garnished with wildflowers of every hue of the rainbow. You can see lupines, brodea, golden poppies, shooting stars, redbud, columbines and so many more varieties that you can't even identify them all.

How about the fishing? I'd love to tell you it's fantastic, but it's really pretty slow. There's just too much water for even great anglers to cope. Oh, there are a few small streams that are fishable but you have to fight a tangle of branches overhead and a jungle of blackberries underfoot.

The best advice I could give you right now is to load up your camera, bring lots of extra film, and enjoy the splendor of one of the most beautiful spots on earth. I wouldn't want to be accused of encouraging anyone to play hooky from church, but at least for me, no finer cathedral exists anywhere on earth. I always come away with my batteries recharged and a deeper conviction that the awe inspiring waterfalls and the intricate beauty of the tiniest wildflowers could not have been just a gigantic molecular accident. Surely, the hand of God has been at work here.

I suspect that I and most of my fellow outdoors fanatics are not really out there for the meat, or fish we sometimes bring home, but rather for the experience of it all. Try a trip to Yosemite and see if you don't agree.

⌘ ⌘ ⌘

FLY FISHING MYTHS

July 2003

One of my pet peeves is the myth that seems to surround flyfishing. Actually, there is a series of myths tied to the sport, all of which are hogwash. The idea that flyfishing is difficult is especially bothersome to me. I learned to flyfish as a child and never even realized that there was another way to catch trout until I was about 10 years old. Of course we fished for bass and panfish with conventional spinning and baitcasting gear and used worms and minnows as bait. I just never made the connection that you could use anything other than a fly for trout. Actually, fly fishing is extremely easy, and I can have almost any schmuck catching trout on a fly with less than an hour's instruction.

Another myth associated with flyfishing is that it is expensive and that only rich Harvard graduates can afford it. Again nothing could be further from the truth. A lifetime ago, I worked as a construction laborer helping to build a ski resort in the Sierra Nevada. For my lunch, I carried a coil of 10 pound test leader material and half dozen flies in my shirt pocket. At noon, I would cut a 6 or 7 foot alder branch for a rod, and tie on the leader and a fly. I fished a brushy little creek near the construction site and could usually catch 5 or 6 brook trout in a half hour. By building a small fire on a streamside sandbar, and whittling my alder rod into a roasting stick, I could cook my catch and complete lunch in an hour or less. No, flyfishing doesn't have to be expensive.

Like anything else in life there are always two sides to any story. You can spend lots of money on flyfishing if you want to, but you don't have to. I have purchased fancy graphite rods and expensive flylines. Heck, I have even bought flies from the expensive outfits like Orvis, but quite truthfully, I prefer to use my own flies tied from barnyard chicken feathers, and road killed critters. I have, on occasion, hired a fishing guide and float-fished some famous trout river, but I'm really more comfortable wading the Stanislaus or the Tuolumne. While I do own an expensive pair of chest waders, 90% of the time I wade wet in old Levis. Yes, flyfishing can be expensive, but only if you want it to be.

Another BS myth that annoys me is that you have to be really smart or well educated to be a flyfisher. Some uppity flyfishers perpetuate that myth and try to impress people by using Latin names for the bugs that trout eat. You can indeed catch some nice trout using an imitation of the *Pteronarcys Californica*, but all you really need to know is that you want to tie on a black wooly worm when the trout are eating black bugs. Along the same lines, if you're fishing a grassy meadow stream in mid summer, you really don't need to know that *Plecoptera* is the Latin name for a stonefly. All you have to know is to tie on a grasshopper fly. It's not really rocket science. Is it fun to learn all the scientific names? Yeah, but it's not a real necessity.

Don't let all the myths get in the way of having a great time. Flyfishing is simple, affordable, and great fun. To learn more, consult your local library, or contact one of the area flyfishing shops.

⌘ ⌘ ⌘

Monty Wolf's Cabin 1971

THE LEGEND OF MONTY WOLF

November 2008

Part of the legacy of any region is the compilation of verbal history of the area. The great outdoors plays a vibrant part in such oral histories. Every once in awhile someone comes along and records such tales in any given area. Sometimes the main focus of the stories is a real person and sometimes they are completely fictional. The mighty logger Paul Bunyan, cowboy Pecos Bill, and rail driver John Henry are fictional characters who come to mind, while Jesse James and Billie the Kid were real, breathing people. Some local legends seem to be a mixture of truth and fiction. One such example is the legend of Monty Wolf.

Monty Wolf was an old Indian (or a Gringo who claimed to be Indian) who lived in what is now called the Mokelumne Wilderness. He built at least two cabins way back in the woods, as far from humanity as possible. That he was a real person is not in doubt; I have personally met several people who knew him, although there aren't very many still alive. Monty was a hermit who survived by guiding a few fishermen in the summer and hunters in the fall. His few contacts with the outside world were limited to the occupants of cabins and businesses along Ebbetts Pass.

There were a host of tales about Monty Wolf that are told around the campfires along Highway 4. All seemed to agree that Monty was originally from "Back East," wherever that was. Some tales had it that Monty had killed a fellow and fled west into the most remote wilderness to avoid prosecution. Other tales had Monty pegged as a draft dodger from World War I.

In addition to his income from guiding hunters and fishermen, legend had it that Monty sort of helped himself to the contents of backwoods cabins that were unused for the winter. Since locking your cabin really didn't help much, most property owners just left their cabins unlocked for the winter and avoided fixing broken doors and such. There was a tale about a fellow who bought a nice new picnic table with attached benches. Not wanting his fancy table to disappear over the winter, the fellow attached it to a giant tree with a huge log chain. Next spring, the property owner returned to find that his giant tree had been cut down and his table and log chain were both missing.

Some of the tales of Monty wolf chronicled his generosity or his incredible stamina. I recall the matriarch of a pioneer cattle family relating how Monty Wolf would leave a mess of freshly cleaned trout in her evaporative cooler whenever he was in the neighborhood. Whether or not the Monty Wolf stories were true, I don't know for sure. But I do know that I visited Monty Wolf's cabin and saw a big fancy picnic table with a huge log chain still attached.

Depending upon who you listened to, Monty Wolf just disappeared somewhere in the late 1940's or early 1950's. Even though Monty Wolf was gone, his cabins still remained. His upper cabin was about a 4 mile hike down the Mokelumne River Canyon from Hermit Valley near the top of Ebbetts Pass. Monty Wolf's cabin sat in a small glade about 100 yards back from the Mokelumne River. The glade was filled with ferns that were waist high and a small unnamed feeder stream flowed by the cabin.

The cabin itself was exactly what you'd picture if you closed your eyes and tried to imagine one. It had log walls, laid right on the ground. There was a single door that you had to duck through to enter, and one small window that faced the northern winter sun was all that let in light to the tiny cabin. On the outside, the cabin was roofed with pieces tin from square 5 gallon cans that had been flattened out and nailed to the roof. Inside the cabin, you could see the roof poles that the tin cans had been nailed to. On the wall at the far end of the cabin hung a couple old calendars from the 1930's.

Nearby was Monty Wolf's one concession to luxury—a two-hole outhouse. I still can't figure out why he needed a two-hole outhouse. All in all, it was a wilderness experience that evoked memories of a time that was no more, a time when there was still a frontier where a man could get a new start.

Unfortunately, sometime in the late 60's or early 70's some-one from the government decided that such relics were an intrusion into a wilderness area and Monty Wolf's cabin was burned to the ground. Apparently, there was a con-certed program to remove such "intrusions" and there was a regular person assigned to cabin removal. Forest Service personnel even had a derogatory nickname for the guy on cabin removal detail; they called him "Harry the Torch" or some such nonsense. You'd think that such a policy would be insane wouldn't you? What right thinking person would willingly destroy the last vestiges of our frontier past? Now only Monty Wolf's lower cabin remains. Whatever your ex-cuse to get outdoors and enjoy the marvels that abound is OK with me, but if you happen to be a history buff, that's a good reason too. Get out there and enjoy!

⌘ ⌘ ⌘

DON'T GO OFF HALF-COCKED

June 2009

Language is a strange device. Lord only knows how many weird phrases we learned as children. You know, useful stuff like, "You'd better watch your Ps and Qs," or "He's the spitting image of his father."

Naturally, many of these phrases grew out of simpler times. "Spitting image" evolved from the phrase that someone represented both the "spirit and image" of a parent or other ancestor and that somehow evolved into spitting image. A fairly common phrase that mystifies many folks is the admonition not to go off half-cocked. Although I definitely got the impression that going off half-cocked was a bad idea, I never really gave much thought to why being half-cocked was undesireable, until last weekend when I sat in on a hunter safety class sponsored by Bass Pro Shops in Manteca.

I took my first hunter safety course along with my brother when we were kids. It was required if you wanted to get a hunting license, and we were taught the basics of gun safety. A decade or so later as part of Big Brothers of America, I again attended hunter safety classes to accompany my "little brother," Billy, so that he and I could go hunting together. Some of the techniques had changed but the basic message remained constant—safety, safety, safety. A decade or so ago, my son and I attended hunter safety classes at the Ripon High School rifle range. Can you imagine that? A rifle range at a high school! Amazingly enough there have been no mass killings in Ripon and those evil guns don't seem to have made Ripon a terrible place. Quite the contrary, Ripon may well be one of the safest towns in the valley despite all our guns.

For Christmas I had signed my son-in law, Jonathan, up for hunter safety classes at Bass Pro, and there was a 6 month waiting list to get into class. I thought it would be interesting to see what sort of new-fangled teaching aides were now being used to teach the old message of gun safety. I envisioned all sorts of computer Power Point presentations, laser simulators, and other state of the art goodies. Guess what, we got to sit at tables and study nicely illustrated comic books and learn: safety, safety, safety. There was no high tech stuff at all. The instructor, however, did a pretty darned good job of making hunter safety interesting. The course now includes sections on archery safety and even instruction on safety with muzzle loading guns that shoot black powder.

A cardinal rule was that there would be no live ammunition in class, but the students got to handle all sorts of guns to familiarize themselves with their safe use. There were the expected young boys eager to become hunters like their dads and a couple teen girls who wanted to hunt with their boyfriends. Interestingly, there were also single women who'd never held a gun, as well as retired old guys who wanted to take up shooting for the first time.

We learned how to safely handle every sort of gun imaginable: single shot, lever action, bolt actions, semi-autos, double barrels, and revolvers. We learned how to check the action to see that a gun is empty and then memorized the eternal rule that you treat every gun as if it's always loaded. We learned to be sure of your backstop behind your target and how to carry your gun with the muzzle pointing in a safe direction.

We also learned that with the old cowboy-style single action revolver and with some models of rifles and shotguns that some folks would pull the hammer back to a half-cocked position and think that the gun was safe to carry. Hence the phrase to "go off half-cocked." The problem is that the gun at half-cock can fire if it is dropped or if something strikes the hammer.

I had a farmer friend who used to carry a break action shotgun at half-cock on his tractor while working his orchards. Somehow the gun fell and the hammer hit a tire lug which fired the shotgun right into his guts. Doctors at the emergency room were unable to save him, and it took him several hours to die.

There are 80 million gun owners in the United States, and each year there are less than 1,500 accidental gun deaths. By contrast, there are over 120,000 accidental deaths each year caused by physician mistakes. Neither figure is acceptable. We must constantly keep on guard to avoid accidents so that our lives can be as safe as we can make them. Gun owners suffer from the same basic problem as physicians—they come from the human race. Because we are human, we will undoubtedly make mistakes, but whether we are physicians or firefighters or fry cooks, we must always strive to make our families safe.

Over the past 50 years or so, hunter safety has achieved remarkable success. Even if you don't hunt, you should consider taking an NRA approved hunter safety course. Go down to Bass Pro, or the Barnwood, or any local gun shop and inquire about safety courses. You're never too old to learn this stuff. Firing a round of sporting clays is sort of like playing golf with a shotgun. You shoot from different angles and distances. Target shooting is a great challenge, and even plinking cans with a 22 is just plain fun. Hunting will get you closer to nature and closer to the family members you hunt with. But the most important part of all is to do it safely. Don't go off half-cocked.

⌘ ⌘ ⌘

Wilderness Hot Tub
Mammoth Lakes, California

WILDERNESS HOT TUBS

July 2009

While *Tight Lines* is primarily an outdoor column focusing on fishing and hunting, there are an amazing number of fascinating and beautiful outdoor wonders out there for the outdoors enthusiast to enjoy. A great example is the numerous hot springs that are plentiful all over the west. Perhaps my first exposure to hot springs as a child was the Grover Hot Springs State Park near Markleville in Alpine County where my family vacationed every summer.

Naturally, I'm not alone in my fascination with hot springs. What seems like a lifetime ago, I taught a course in archeology at Delta College. One of the sites we explored was the Byron Hot Springs about 20 miles west of Tracy on Byron Road. Long before Columbus arrived in the New World, California Indians were occupying Byron Hot Springs. They even buried their dead in the hot springs and the bones that remained became encrusted with black and yellow mineral deposits.

We also observed a burial practice we'd never seen elsewhere: numerous burials where the head of the deceased rested upon a stone pestle which was broken in half in every instance. Why? *Quien sabe?* Perhaps to signify the end of the life cycle. We simply don't know. What we do know was that hot springs have been revered as special places by people of many cultures since before recorded history began.

Another fascinating place to experience hot springs is in the Mammoth Lakes area on the east slope of the Sierra Nevada. Hot Creek, just east of the town of Mammoth

Lakes is famous for its trophy trout fishing. One of the qualities of hot springs is that the hot water dissolves large quantities of minerals deep beneath the earth. When the hot water reaches the surface, the minerals begin to deposit along the edges of the hot springs. In addition, the mineral laden waters once sufficiently cooled, caused abnormally fast growth rates in the trout that resided there. The result? A special bonus for trout fishers: huge trout from small streams!

Another reputed benefit of hot springs is that they may have medicinal or curative properties. As far back as the ancient Romans, hot springs were popular for relieving the stress of daily life. The redwood hot tubs of the 60s hippies were not exactly a new phenomenon. In fact the hot tub craze is still with us, but has developed an outdoors twist. Almost everywhere there are remote wilderness hot springs, there are hand made hot tubs constructed out of local materials. Some enterprising soul has taken a couple hundred feet of pipe, or dug a couple hundred feet of ditch, to channel the flow of a hot spring to a rock drop-off of several feet. The water has now cooled from boiling to relaxingly hot. A tub is fashioned using rocks and mortar and the water flows into the wilderness hot tub. Often times there is an outlet pipe with a tennis ball for a plug, you can remove the tennis ball, drain the tub and replace it so that now you have a fresh tub filled with refreshing hot water.

The wilderness hot tubs are scattered all over the desert in hot spring country. To find them, you go for a drive in the sagebrush in hot spring country. Go early in the morning when the surrounding air is cold and look for steam rising up out of the sagebrush. Sometimes you may find the hot spring itself, other times you may find the hot tub made by fellow desert rats. Once you have found your secret desert spa, camp nearby, but not too close, because, at dark, desert dwellers may mysteriously appear. The desert dwellers may be human, and they may not. If you're lucky, you may share your desert spa with bunnies, foxes, and coyotes underneath an incredible display of nighttime stars.

⌘ ⌘ ⌘

Old Methodist Church, Bodie Ca

GHOST TOWNS

January 2010

Saw a piece on the TV news the other day about Bodie, the ghost town on the very east border of California. Bodie is a delightful experience and I heartily recommend that you visit it. It is a ghost town that is still largely intact and left just as it was when its miners abandoned it. I actually knew a guy who may have been one of the last people who lived in Bodie. Jack was the son of a mining engineer who worked in Bodie just about the time the gold ran out. There are still whiskey bottles in the old saloons, wagons in the livery stables, and coffins in the undertaker's parlor. It really tugs at your heart when you see a child's coffin, and it hits you that there were real families with moms and dads and kids who lived, played and died there.

One of the fringe benefits of constantly searching for the next undiscovered fishing spot, or secret hunting hotspot is that along the way you stumble across ghost towns and mining camps that were scattered all over the western U.S. It seems crazy, but ghost towns can turn up almost anywhere. Growing up in Tracy, almost everyone had patios, barbeques, and walkways made from Carnegie Bricks. Folks from would drive their truck out to Carnegie and fill it with bricks from the old collapsed brick buildings. As kids we delighted in exploring old mines and abandoned lumber camps. They were living history lessons and with a little imagination you found yourself back in the 1850s along with the loggers and miners.

I recall a giant railroad trestle that spanned the junction of two Sierra Nevada creeks. It must have been 50 feet above the creek and was still intact with supports, ties, rails and even water tanks that used to fill the steam engines. My brother and I would play for hours beneath the spout of a redwood water tank as though it was our own personal shower. The coal mine at Tesla was about 5 miles west of Carnegie and was a huge complex of tunnels, shafts and drifts dug by the miners in search of fuel for the trains and ships that powered the west. We would wander around inside that mountain for hours, and amazingly we never got killed or even seriously hurt, although there was no doubt that our moms truly earned their grey hairs.

For the most part, the ghost towns that remain are now state parks and pretty carefully preserved and regulated. That is both the good news and the bad. You can't walk into the firehouse of a ghost town anymore and roll the horse-drawn fire engine out into the street to have your picture taken for posterity.

Now you get to look at the old relic through a plexiglass box so that curious little hands can no longer feel the rough grain of the weathered sides. While the relics are preserved in their nice displays you can't blow off the dust and smell the inside of an old dynamite box. Kids can no longer explore the Tesla mines because they might disturb the bat habitat. I know such rules are necessary to save the old treasures, but somehow today's kids are missing out, and they don't even know it.

Believe it or not, there are still ghost towns, mining camps, and logging camps that are lost in the mists of time. They are still out there and you can still find them once in a rare while if you try. I can take you to a mine today that still has a working ventilation system made from a washtub ingeniously turned into a weathervane that still rotates into the wind and blows fresh air deep into the mine. The creaking of that washtub weathervane is a haunting song that still sings in the desert wind. There are mine tunnels out there complete with ore cars that still roll on their tracks and the rock face of the mine still has a star drill waiting for the next sledgehammer blow to deepen the hole for the dynamite charge that will never come.

If you really try, you can still find these portals to the past. With a little research, a lot of miles on your 4 wheel drive, and a lot of wear on your shoes, there are still ghost towns waiting for you. Be advised though, the ghost town bug is addicting. Once you start, you can't quit.

Where do you start? Why, at the local library of course. Check out books on ghost towns of the west, California ghost towns and logging camps, Nevada ghost towns. Let your imagination run wild, read everything you can find. Consult your reference librarian at your local library; they love to help and they love a challenge. Once you've studied possible locations, wait for a sunny weekend and go off in search of your very own El Dorado.

⌘ ⌘ ⌘

Section Three

FAMILY

WHY A WILD RIVER

April 1984

One doesn't have to have known me very long to figure out that not only am I a fanatical trout fisher, but also that I prefer to seek my elusive quarry in the wildest and most remote locations. Even stranger to some people I know, is the fact that I spend a lot of what could otherwise be productive fishing time doing conservation work to save my favorite wild trout stream, the Tuolumne River. Often my non-angling friends, and even some fishing friends, will ask why I waste so much time on an activity that costs me money rather than makes it, and that creates tension rather than relieves it.

Why can't I be satisfied fishing for catfish in the San Joaquin Delta, or trolling for salmon at the mouth of the American? If I must pursue trout, what's wrong with joining the many dry fly anglers from all over the world who converge upon famous Hat Creek to cast delicate imitations of tiny mayflies to wary, sophisticated trout? After all, even a novice flyfisher knows that it's the height of challenge to skillfully outwit an old trout that has spent its entire life evading the tempting offerings of a parade of anglers.

Why, indeed, can't I be satisfied with joining the hordes of my angling brethren and sistren? After considerable thought, I've concluded that the reason I prefer wilderness angling is the very absence of other anglers. Sure, I enjoy going out in the Delta with a couple of friends, a cribbage board, and a six pack, but for serious fishing, there are just too many people. I'm afraid that if I cast my line way out where the big ones bite, I'll decapitate some poor water skier with my line. Yes, I also enjoy trolling for salmon, but when the salmon are running, there are so many boats congregated at the hot spots that you have to be constantly alert lest you have a mid-stream collision. It's like fishing in rush hour traffic. Even my fellow trout anglers seem to be afflicted with what I call crowditis. Roadside waters are so crowded on the opening day of trout season that you almost have to bring your own rock just to have a place to stand.

If I am a fanatic about angling solitude, it's because its part of a family tradition handed down from one generation to another. Back when Teddy Roosevelt was President, my grandfather was fishing in the solitude of Colorado's wilderness. He taught my father to fish in the backcountry streams of the High Sierra. When my brother and I were young, Dad would lead us into remote canyons where we often fished all day without seeing another angler.

Although we never suspected it at the time, those lonely canyons were classrooms where we learned subjects not covered in school. We learned conservation ethics from tiptoeing out on a giant boulder to watch Dad carefully east into a pool so clear it seemed devoid of water. Year after year we would come to this pool where Dad would cast to his favorite trout, a monster fish he called Big Mack, long before that name became a symbol of our throw-away fast-food culture. From out of nowhere a giant trout would materialize and race upward to engulf Dad's fly. Usually the fight lasted only the split second it took Big Mack to change direction and vanish into the ether from whence he came.

Sometimes, however, Dad would keep him on long enough to entice him to leap clear of the water, surrounded by a halo of droplets sparkling in the sun. Dad never caught Big Mack, but he always said that it didn't matter because he'd just have to release him anyway. A fish that incredible, we learned, belonged alive and free in his stream, not gathering dust on someone's wall.

Those lonely Sierra canyons also taught us our heritage. Passing abandoned mining and logging camps while fishing, there was always time to admire the ingenuity and perseverance of the people who built them. We used to take showers under the spouts of water tanks that still worked long after the logging railroads were abandoned. We learned natural history first hand from eagles, mountain lions and bear droppings so fresh they still had steam rising from them.

So, why do I angle for wild trout on wilderness streams? Perhaps in part because I long to maintain the roots to my past. Perhaps because my blood pressure drops every time I'm out on the stream. Maybe because it's refreshing to fish for unsophisticated trout that impulsively smash into a fly with the same abandon their ancestors had. Who knows? Maybe I frequent wild places because I like to see a mink searching for food, or perhaps I enjoy the thrill of seeing a coiled rattlesnake lying in deadly, yet beautiful repose.

I suppose any of those reasons would be sufficient cause to spend time trying to preserve what few wild places are left. I suspect, however, that the most important reason I invest time in trying to save rivers is just across the typewriter from me. My little girl, Julie, is sitting on the floor playing with her crayons, drawing Thanksgiving turkeys. I want her to be able to see real wild turkeys, and real eagles, and bears and mining ruins, just as I did. But more than almost anything in the world, I'd like for Julie to be able to recall, in her mind's eye, a magnificent, eternal Big Mack, suspended in a halo of water droplets above a stream that flows wild forever. Julie, I do it for you.

⌘ ⌘ ⌘

OUTDOOR GIFT TRADITIONS

December 2005

Well, it's that time of year again when people start going crazy buying gifts for Christmas. Don't get me wrong, I love Christmas and the celebration of Christ's Birth. I also like giving and getting gifts, but think maybe we've gotten a little carried away with it all. These days I'm trying to put in a little thought and give gifts that will be more suited to the individual recipient. I suppose a Christmas tree neck tie or a stale fruitcake is all right, but a gift that the recipient can use might be much better received. Here's an idea that might bring back some of the real meaning of Christmas gifts. Why not create a Christmas tradition that is your very own?

If you've got a spouse who likes to fish, get him a fishing license for the coming year. You don't have to worry about getting the right size, or color or line weight. One size fits all, ands it's a gift they can use all year long. Every time I go fishing I can think of my wife who has bought my fishing license. My son-in law is in law enforcement and regularly shoots a handgun to stay proficient. Every year, he gets a small box that is very heavy and feels like lead. No, it's not too big a surprise and every year he picks up the heavy little box and says, "Gee, I wonder what this is?"

Some traditions can be passed from one generation to another. In 1977, I bought my dad a nice pocket knife and then spent several hours creating a specially wrapped box which I made by cutting out fishing scenes from outdoor magazines and decorating every surface of the box with them. Dad was more delighted with the box than with the knife inside. The next year I made another special fishing scene box for Dad, but was really surprised when I received a gift from him in the box I had given him the year before. Every year thereafter Dad and I would exchange our recycled boxes covered with leaping trout, and sparkling waterfalls. We both knew what the box contained, but somehow that wasn't the point. Our dumb fishing Christmas boxes had become a tradition more important than any physical gift could ever be.

Now as Christmas draws near, I select a knife with care, and wrap it in old news paper from 1977 or 1978 and place it in a gaudy box from the closet shelf that I've dusted off with care. Sometimes I get a little teary-eyed trying to seal the recycled box, because it brings back of a flood memories of Dad and I fishing together. Dad has gone on to that big Trout Stream in the Sky, only now I give the fishing box to my son and an old tradition continues, but with another generation.

You too could create your own family tradition. It doesn't have to be like mine, in fact it probably shouldn't be. If your loved one is an artist, maybe you could give a new camel hair brush each year, If photography is your spouses passion, perhaps a couple rolls of super fast film, for low-light shots would be ideal, or an extra memory card for a digital camera. For general nature enthusiasts, one of those new digital trail cameras could be just the ticket. They shoot both still and video shots are equipped with motion sensors to trigger the photo, and work both day and night. They take some amazing wildlife shots while you are snuggled up next to a cozy fire.

Whatever outdoor pursuit lights a fire for the person you care about, there lies the germ of a great outdoor tradition in gift giving. Just remember, that the gift isn't the important thing. It's the idea that you care enough to select just the perfect one. Give it a try, this year you might just begin a tradition that will last for generations.

⌘ ⌘ ⌘

THE RANGER FROM HELL

June 1995

Last year, Wayne Shockey and I took our boys on a camping trip to the Mammoth Lakes area. One of the days we were camped at Devils Postpile National Monument. We hadn't thought to make prior reservations and were forced to camp in a crowded area. We had just finished breakfast and went down to the creek to try our luck at fishing.

Upon our return to camp we found two rangers waiting for us. They asked us if this was our camp and when we replied that it was, they informed us that we needed to be a little more careful with our food storage because the bears were getting smarter and smarter. Actually, the rangers were right when they chastised us, we had left our ice chests out in plain sight and some of the boys hadn't done a thorough job cleaning all the food residue off their breakfast dishes. Even though it was mid morning in a crowded campground with people everywhere, it was like an open invitation for bears.

What impressed me though was that the rangers had good people skills and took the time to explain to us what we were doing wrong, and how to correct the situation so that we would avoid bear problems in the future. The rangers handled themselves professionally, and I am still singing the praises of the Mammoth Lakes area. The rangers at Devils Postpile deserve a pat on the back for turning a potentially difficult situation into a public relations plus.

Ironically, it was a similar incident near the town of Independence involving bear safety, campers, and a ranger who apparently had very poor people skills which triggered my recollection of the skilled rangers. I got a call last week from a cousin of mine who has been an outdoor enthusiast for all of his 50 + years. Harvey Moyer takes an annual back packing trip with one or both of his daughters, his nephew, and an assortment of neighborhood kids and their parents. Year after year Harvey leads his youthful crew into the back country where they hike, fish, and sing around the campfire. This year however their trip was ruined, not by bears, bees, or broken bones, but by bureaucracy in the form of the Ranger from Hell.

As near as I can tell, it all began when Harvey's daughter Sarah and one of her girlfriends were hiking near their campsite. They were stopped by a ranger who asked where they were camped, and if they had bear boxes to store their food in. Bear boxes are bear proof containers that you can purchase for camping food storage. The girls replied that they didn't have bear boxes but that they stored their food the old fashioned way by suspending it out of bear range with a rope. The ranger replied that the old way wasn't good enough and without bear boxes they'd have to pack up and leave immediately.

The girls returned to camp and told Harvey about the ranger who demanded they leave immediately because they had no bear boxes. Harvey decided there was no way he was going to lead a bunch of kids down a mountain trail on foot at night. Big mistake, Harv! Little did he know that he was up against a bureaucrat determined to flex her administrative muscles and show these unrepentant campers a thing or two.

As they were eating dinner the ranger strode into camp and demanded to know why they hadn't left as she had ordered. Harvey explained his rationale about hiking in the dark, but that only served to enrage the mountain martinet. She demanded to see their wilderness permit and Harvey explained that they had left for their camping trip right after work and when they arrived at the ranger station in the middle of the night the box with the permit forms was empty. Rather than wait until the ranger station opened the next morning Harvey decided to drive on to make the trailhead by dawn. On the way to their camp, they hiked past a sign which admonished "no dogs allowed," which was no problem because they didn't bring a dog. He confessed that he had no wilderness permit but that he thought that was no worse a transgression than the ranger having a dog and ignoring the no dog mandate. His observation did not set well. Immediately the ranger began writing a citation for camping without a wilderness permit, price tag - $100. I guess there is no fine for violation of the "no dog" rule if you're a ranger. Upon issuing her citation the ranger departed with the admonition that they'd better leave first thing next morning, or else.

Sometime later, after dinner, the group tried to forget the unpleasant incident, and enjoy the last of their trip with some traditional camp singing. Screwed up again, Harv! How dare you try to have fun after you've been busted. The ranger materialized from the darkness to warn the campers that they were making too much noise. After quieting the singers down, Harvey mentioned to the ranger that they were in a remote area, not a busy campground, and he saw nothing wrong with singing after dinner. This apparently irritated the ranger who proceed to write Harvey another citation (for improper food storage), price tag - $25.

The next morning Harvey and the kids went to extra special pains to make sure their camp was picked up cleaner than it was when they found it. He told the kids to be sure they gave the ranger no reason whatsoever to bust them a third time. Once they had their campsite in spotless condition they packed on down the hill to the trailhead thinking their troubles were all behind them. Wrong again, Harv! Never underestimate the power of an angered bureaucrat. The next week in the mail Harvey got a citation for "leaving garbage, refuse or debris" at a campsite, price tag - $50.

Now he's really mad. But what can he do about it? The address where you mail your fines is in Atlanta or somewhere and if he wants to fight the tickets he's got to take 2 days off work and drive 300 miles each way to court. Poor old Harvey is stuck between a rock and a hard place He could call the Chamber of Commerce in Independence and tell them that he'll never camp in the area again, but what good will that do? I guess he could call his congress member, but can a congress member actually have any impact on the Secretary of Agriculture? Who knows? If any of you have any brilliant ideas, about a solution to Harvey's problem, let me know. It sounds to me as though he ran into The Ranger from Hell.

⌘ ⌘ ⌘

THE LEGACY

March 2004

Several years ago I wrote a column entitled "Angling Antiques" in which I described the contents of an unknown angler's tackle box and what it told me about him. I had been fortunate enough to obtain both the tackle box and a couple of antique bamboo rods and was fascinated by the story they told.

Recently I received a similar legacy, which had much more sentimental value. Just before Christmas, my father had suffered a series of strokes that made it necessary for him to enter a convalescent hospital for the rest of his life. Dad suffered severe brain damage and dementia and can never go home again. Some days, I don't think he even recognizes me. Mom gave me Dad's old fishing gear since he won't be using it again. This time, as I went through an old anglers gear, it wasn't just an interesting exercise, but was a personal and gut wrenching experience.

As I went through Dad's stuff, it spoke volumes to me. His fishing vest was serviceable, but not fancy, made by Columbia Sportswear, not Eddie Bauer, or Abercrombie and Fitch. Attached to the outside by a sturdy shoelace, was his fish counter, which he flicked every time he caught and released another trout. At the end of the day he might have two or three fish in his creel, but there were 40 or 50 that he had released. Also hanging from the outside of the vest was his folding scissors with which he would snip lines and leaders during a days fishing.

One of the larger vest pockets held a plastic rotary fly box with several dozen flies that Dad had tied. It evoked memories of sitting around the house on a rainy winter night tying flies in front of the fireplace. We would gather up all the little bits of fur, and thread, and feathers that we generated in an evening and toss them in the fireplace before going to bed. In other, battered aluminum fly boxes were more dozens of flies, most of which were his favorite pattern, the Wooly Worm, Oh sure, Dad had most of the other patterns like the Adams, or Mosquito, or the Royal Coachman, but his tried and true favorite was the old Wooly Worm.

Naturally, Dad had several reels but his favorite was a double action reel that you could use as an automatic and just push a lever to take in line, or you could use the handle and crank in line manually if you chose. The dual action reel was only made by one company, Ocean City, and when they went out of business, he bought a half dozen reels so that he'd never be without his favorite reel. Ordinarily a good reel will last a lifetime, but Dad just wanted to be sure.

Another vest pocket held his folding aluminum cup that evoked images of stops to rest at nameless side streams along the long hot climb out of so many Sierra canyons. It seems the fishing is always better when you walk past the crowds into the backcountry. Instead of eight or ten fish a day, our average was in the dozens because Dad would insist we walk until we were alone. Dad always thought that trout fishing should be a solitary pursuit, just between you and the fish.

Other vest pockets included indispensable items like toilet paper, soap, bug repellant, reel grease, and line grease to make your line float. Naturally, there were extra leaders, a sharpening stone for knives and hooks, and a match safe to keep your matches dry. Tucked in the big pocket in the back of his vest was a folding net housed in a leather holster that you'd wear on your belt. Alongside the folding net was a plastic rain poncho that was sometimes worth its weight in gold.

As I look at the inventory of the gear I had inherited, almost every item evoked memories of streams and fish and adventures that stretched over the fifty years or so that I could remember. The match safe reminded me of a rainy day in the mid 1950s when Dad found a big overhanging rock along the Tuolumne River and made a roaring fire so that my brother and I could stay warm and dry while Dad fished in the rain. The fish counter reminded me of the day on Cherry Creek when I caught and released 106 trout while my darned partner caught 156 fish!

Dads hook sharpener reminded me of the time we were fishing the Mokelumne near Monty Wolf's cabin, and I missed hooking almost 20 fish in a row. When we realized that my hook had broken just past the bend, we had a good laugh at my mistake. Even his little hotel sized bar of soap reminded me of the time I was 5 years old and had gotten lost along the Tuolumne for several hours. When Dad finally found me, he sat me down beside the stream and washed away my tears with that bar of soap. Somehow, everything seemed better after that.

It's really amazing how many memories could be wrapped up in a bunch of old fishing gear. I recall when Dad was setting up his trust, I told him I really didn't want his money, that he should spend it on himself and Mom. I said that I would however like to have his fishing gear when he could use it. It won't buy me a condo in Baja, but that old battered fishing gear is just about the best legacy I could hope for. During the recent past, I have taken my son fishing on many of the streams I fished with my Dad. Hopefully, I can leave my son with an enduring love of God's creation; if I can, he will receive the kind of legacy that money can't buy. Maybe someday, he'll feel as I do now. Thanks for the legacy, Dad.

⌘ ⌘ ⌘

THE IRON KETTLE
Circa 1810 to 1856

THE IRON KETTLE

March 2007

Oftentimes when you're out afield, you happen across things that may have no bearing upon hunting or fishing but which enhance the overall outdoor experience. The iron kettle is a perfect example. For decades my Dad and I fished a particular stretch of stream that had great fishing largely because it was difficult to get to. We walked down a trail that followed the main river for 2 miles and then fished up a tributary creek about 4 miles to an old immigrant road that was abandoned in 1858. We walked back 4 more miles along the route of the old immigrant road to our camp. Because there was no marked trail and it was an all day excursion, we never saw another angler and had the stream all to ourselves.

The walk back was a tiring one but somehow it was always worth the effort. One such walk, in 1980, brought an extra bonus in the form of an old rusty iron kettle that my father found along the immigrant road. The old kettle was partially buried in dirt and leaves and as he brushed off the dirt, Dad could see it was completely intact, including the bail and lid. The maker's name was cast in the iron lid, B. Ellis and Co, S. Carver, Mass.

When Dad returned to camp that night with the iron kettle, I could almost imagine it falling off the back of an immigrant family's wagon. Since the stretch of road it was found on was only in use for two years, we can be pretty sure was lost in 1857 or 1858. If only it could talk, I wondered what tales the kettle would tell. With a little research, the old kettle began to weave its story. Little did I know that it would talk directly to me.

Carver, Massachusetts, lies about 10 miles from Plymouth Rock where the Pilgrims landed in 1620 and has been inhabited since 1637. Shortly after the American Revolution, a foundry was built which operated in Carver until 1910. It provided shot for the new country in the war of 1812 and cannons for the Yankees in the Civil War. In 1810, the Federal Foundry was purchased by Benjamin Ellis and renamed. After the War of 1812, the B. Ellis and Co foundry became known far and wide as a maker of cast iron kettles and cast iron stoves. To this day, there is an iron kettle on the Carver Town Seal. The company owner, Benjamin Ellis, died in 1856 and the foundry changed names again. Thus our kettle was manufactured sometime between 1810 and 1856.

The old iron kettle resided beside my parent's fireplace for over 25 years and was an interesting relic of the American westward migration. In the early 1990's my wife Mary became enchanted by the study of genealogy and she's become quite an expert in the field, tracing our family roots back many generations. It's a fascinating field, genealogy, and really helps you appreciate the journey that our ancestors made so that ultimately we would wind up here in California. It's a story of families coming together and striking out westward for a better life for their children and grandchildren. It's a story of families from diverse backgrounds and countries becoming one new American people.

Many times in this column, I have alluded to how the outdoors has provided a common bond in families that has been passed from generation to generation. When I was first married, I was eager to share my love of the outdoors with my bride. We went camping at almost every opportunity, backpacked into the wilderness, and sat around the campfire with my parents watching stars. Poor Mary fell almost as madly in love with the outdoors as I did. In time, our children learned the same reverence for wild places. We camp with them and their spouses, and our now grandchildren too, much like our parents did with us a generation before.

"What does all this sentimental stuff have to do with an old iron kettle?" you are probably wondering. A few years ago, Mary and I were sitting at mom's house warming our backs at the fire. Mary glanced down at the old iron kettle and saw the words "B. Ellis and Co, S. Carver, Mass" and exclaimed that her great-great-great grandfather was named Benjamin Ellis! Could it possibly be the same Ellis who manufactured the old iron kettle?

Sure enough, the maker of the iron kettle was indeed a cousin to Mary's ancestor. What an incredible coincidence that almost 200 years ago one of my wife's relatives made a kettle that got lost in the 1850's and then found over 120 years later by my father. What an amazing journey that kettle has made, to travel from Massachusetts by wagon all the way to California, to get lost and then eventually to wind up right back with a relative of the same family that made it.

Shortly after I discovered the history of the kettle, I made my Mom an offer she couldn't refuse. The iron kettle now resides in a place of honor beside our hearth. It seems as though the iron kettle could indeed talk. It tells the story of a nation, of a family, and of a continuing tradition of reverence for God's outdoors.

⌘ ⌘ ⌘

MOM'S HANDGUN

December 2007

The other day I inherited a couple of handguns from my parents. I ended up with Dad's 357 magnum and my Mom's 38 special. My son, Donald, and I went out and fired a few rounds through each gun. Both guns performed admirably and the bullets went where you aimed them. Dad's 357 was almost like brand new, still in its original box, and with no appreciable wear at all. Mom's Smith and Wesson Airweight in .38 Special however was a different story. It has extensive holster wear and a host of little scratches and dings from about 50 years of use. It's amazing at all of the memories that flood through my mind when I pick up Mom's little Airweight. The moment I touch it, stories of the old gun and its owner jump out at me.

I guess I come from a most atypical family. How many kids grew up with a Mom who packed a handgun? Both Mom and Dad spent almost all of their spare time outdoors. Dad was off fishing and hiking while Mom was out collecting Indian arrowheads. While it's politically incorrect today to collect arrowheads, back then it was a respectable hobby that took Mom into all sorts of remote places. Dad didn't feel that he needed a gun astream, but a woman often alone in the woods found security in having a handgun on her hip. Once, up near the top of Ebbetts Pass Mom was hunting her arrowheads when she came across a large, economy–sized black bear. Mom whipped out her Smith and Wesson Airweight and fired a round into the dirt near the bear's feet. That poor bear probably didn't stop running till he hit the Nevada border. Over the years other bears would feel the sting of gravel from a closely placed bullet if they got to close to Mom or her loved ones.

Another time Mom was wandering along the flats where Elbow Creek joins the Mokelumne River, when she came across lion tracks in the sandy soil. Looking around a little closer, she spotted an adult Mountain Lion perched on a rock about 50 feet away. Again, another bullet carefully placed in the dirt near the big cat and he was off in a flash. Mom never wanted to hurt the bears or cats and was careful only to shoot near enough to pepper them with gravel.

Snakes however, were a different story. Rattlers seemed to be more plentiful on the east slope of the Sierras, as the land fell toward Nevada and the Great Basin. Unfortunately the arrowheading was better on the east slope so that's often where Mom ended up. Whenever she saw a rattler, there was no warning shot and eight times out of ten there was a dead rattler. We still kid Mom about the time she missed and shot off a snake's rattle instead of its head.

Even though she had her share of run-ins with some of God's larger critters, it was the two-legged snakes that were more worrisome. The great outdoors are vast and wonderful with beautiful vistas and fascinating delights to behold. Unfortunately even though God made such magnificent places there was always the danger that Man could foul it up. It wasn't bears or cats, or rattlers that murdered those women up in Yosemite a couple years ago, it was a deranged human. While Mom never had any significant encounter with the dregs of humanity, perhaps it was the fact that she carried her little 38 special that headed off trouble before it started. In all her years of carrying a handgun afield, Mom never had to draw her gun on a fellow human. Perhaps there's merit in the old adage that "an armed society is a polite society."

As Donald and I were trying to punch holes in tin cans with our old inherited guns, a tradition continued of peaceable citizens who perceived guns as neither good nor evil, but simply as tools which can put food on the table, save you from a rattler, or keep some pervert from finding another victim. When we were finished, we packed our antique guns away in their cases, and thanked our lucky stars that we live in a country where we can continue such traditions.

⌘ ⌘ ⌘

RETURN TO TRESTLE CREEK

March 2010

Over 50 years ago my brother, Chris, and I were playing on the huge railroad trestle that spanned the junction of two trout streams in the central Sierra Nevada. The logging railroad had long since been abandoned, but the trestle still remained high above the creek as well as the redwood water tank that filled the long gone steam locomotives.

In 1956 the tank still held water which was piped in by gravity flow from upstream. Dad would let us play among the old logging and railroad ruins while he caught dozens of trout in the creek. We would pull the rope that controlled the fill spout and get hit by a 12 inch wide stream of water. We had a great time playing in the water for several hours until Dad came to chastise us for muddying up his trout stream.

By the 1970's the trestle had been destroyed by fire, and although the old water tank was still standing, it no longer held water. My new bride, Mary, took a picture of me standing alongside the water tank. I was just a young guy in his early 20s. It must have been good timing, because the water tank collapsed into a pile of redwood boards in the next winter's snows.

As the new millennium dawned I was teaching my son, Donald, to fish in the very same stream where my dad had taught my brother and me. There were still a few piles of boards where the loggers cabins had stood, but the forest was inexorably erasing the signs of man's intrusions. Fishing was still just as good as it had always been. You could still catch and release 50 trout a day without too much trouble.

On Father's Day weekend, I decided to return to my old fishing haunts. Since my son was working and couldn't get away, I called my brother's son, Joel Moyer, to see if he wanted to join me. After 50 years there was almost no sign of any human activity at all. The only thing that remained was the creek and the fantastic trout fishing. Joel and I had no trouble catching feisty wild rainbows. Another thing that had changed was that the hills seemed much steeper than before. Or was it that I was 50 years older and 50 pounds heavier?

As we began the drive back to the valley it was comforting to know that while most things are constantly changing, some things remain the same. While man's works crumble back into dust, the wild rainbow trout of Trestle Creek remain as plentiful as ever.

⌘ ⌘ ⌘

VAYA CON DIOS, BRO

October 1999

I've heard it said that we are the sum of the experiences that have shaped us. Thus I guess it makes sense that I equate outdoor activities with family activities. Having been raised in a family where outdoor pursuits were family activities, my earliest memories were of our family doing things together outdoors. Our outdoor activities were not just fair weather expeditions. We had a family tradition that we'd start the New Year off right and every New Years day was spent out in the sun or wind or rain.

In the riparian woods that grew along the San Joaquin River we discovered a concentration of pecan trees and for years we spent New Year's Day and a lot of winter weekend days wandering through the woods gathering up pecans. Then on rainy winter nights we'd have a card table set up near our fireplace where we'd crack pecans near the warmth of the fire. Whenever I eat pecans I think of the rat-a-tat-tat of a woodpecker in the distance or the sting of rain against my face or how good it felt to come home and get warm cracking pecans in front of the fire.

Another favorite family activity was sitting around the summer campfire watching the evening stars and counting man-made satellites as they raced across the nighttime sky. We had brisk competition over who could spot the first satellite of the evening, and who could spot the most. Satellite spottings only counted if you had confirmation from one or more other observers. It seems like our Mom usually won the competition, probably because we kids were too easily distracted by the deer who would come to edge of the campfire light for a handout of day old bread or leftover watermelon rinds. Our favorite was a doe we named Greta who showed up year after year with a succession of fawns in tow.

Some folks might think that outdoor pursuits were male-only activities, but around our camps nothing could be much farther from the truth. We had several families who camped together and the husbands were often back down in the valley working at their jobs. The moms were definitely in charge, and any mom could and did give orders to any kid. I don't know how many times Betty or Marcy told me to go back to the creek again to wash the parts I'd missed.

We took a lot of day trips into some pretty remote country and our moms regularly carried handguns as protection against snakes, bears, and two legged varmints. God help any critter who endangered one of us kids because our moms didn't carry those Chiefs Specials as decorations. We regularly went out to the police range and those women knew how handle a handgun with deadly accuracy. Mom shot the head off more than a few rattlers and chased off several bears over the years by placing a bullet in the dirt between its legs.

It's a good thing our moms were tough because we kids were always into mischief. Nothing bad, mind you, just the sort of things that would give a mom gray hair. Like the time my brother and I caught an owl in an old mine. We managed to get the bird home wrapped in a jacket, and we turned him loose in our garage. We sort of forgot to tell Mom about the owl so it came as a bit of a surprise to her when she went out to the garage in the dark that night and was attacked by something flying out or the darkness at her. Mom got so that she was real cautious checking the pockets of our clothes after she found a bat in my brother's coat pocket, and a horned toad in one of my shirt pockets. Poor Mom.

I guess I was about 11 and my brother was about 8 when we went on a trout fishing expedition on the upper Stanislaus with Dad. I had a brand new pellet gun and Chris had his BB gun. We'd play beside the stream, while Dad would fish upstream for an hour or two and then walk back downstream to us. When Dad returned that afternoon Chris and I had two dead rattlers stretched out over a rock on display. Poor Mom, it's no wonder she has gray hair. The one that bothered her most, I think, was the sign that showed up in our bedroom (on my brother's side, of course) that proclaimed—**DANGER, STAY OFF, THIN ICE**. You can't imagine how loud the sound of cracking ice is.

You might wonder why I'm off on some nostalgia trip about family outdoor activities. I guess it's because our family took a trip last week to Arizona to say good by to my brother. Chris was always a little wilder than I was, and I always figured he'd meet his end via snake bite, gunshot or missing a curve and riding his motorcycle off a cliff. Although he got a Purple Heart from the Marines, he got through Viet Nam OK.

It strikes me as ironic that my baby brother would get done in by something as boring as cancer. For a while we thought he'd be able to beat it, and were looking forward to more trips into the great outdoors together. It would be nice to feel the autumn sun in a pheasant field as we joked about who is the worst shot. It would be swell to count satellites around the campfire one last time, or hear the splash of a rising trout together. But it doesn't look like it's gonna happen. I guess we'll have to be content with the memories we've got.

One day soon, we're going to get the call for another trip to Arizona, and I'm not really looking forward to it. Vaya Con Dios, Bro. We sure had fun while it lasted.

⌘ ⌘ ⌘

Section Four

FISHING

PROSPECTING FOR NEW HOTSPOTS

Jan 20, 1984

I managed to hook some nice trout last Sunday in a small foothill stream that lies at an elevation of 800 feet. The three fish I weighed totaled 4 ½ pounds and averaged 16 inches long. Catching fish that size on a flyrod is a heck of a lot of fun, but you don't have to be a master angler to do it. What you do need to do, however, to catch fish like that is to break out of the conventional thinking we anglers are prone to get into.

Everyone knows that to catch big ones you have to go way back into the boondocks, right? Not necessarily. Usually you have to get to remote areas to catch large trout, it's true. But this is the dead of winter and most anglers aren't even thinking about trout anyway. Large trout that live in reservoirs and lakes are very much like their sea-going cousins, the steelhead. Come the winter rains, and the big fish begin leaving their home lake to travel up tributary streams to spawn. At no other time of year does the average angler stand a better chance of hooking into a large trout.

How do you do it? First get a map or two which shows some of the major reservoirs in your area, and then find tributary streams which enter the lake, preferably ones which are not readily accessible by road. Take your boat across the lake, tie up at the mouth of the stream, then get out and fish up the stream. You might also want to fish the lake right where the stream enters, much like the salmon and steelheaders fish the salt water estuaries. I ask only that you bear one thought in mind, these large fish are spawners so go easy on killing them, and be sure to take only what you can eat.

I grew up trout fishing the streams and rivers of the central Sierras, from the Mokelumne River on the north to the Merced on the south. When I went away to college I was removed from all of my usual streams and had to find new places to fish closer to school. I got maps of the area and began to look for features that resembled streams I was familiar with. For example, low elevation streams will generally be best for late winter and early spring because they won't get all high and muddy from snowmelt like the high country streams.

Another interesting idea when prospecting for new fishing waters is to force yourself not to think like the average angler. For a couple of years, I lived in the San Jose area, and occasionally would take the old Mt. Hamilton Road over through Livermore to get to the valley. On the west slope of Mt. Hamilton the road goes right near a dandy looking bass lake about 75 acres in size that's located in a large county park. The few times I fished it, I ran into several other anglers, and no one seemed to do very well. One day, I was coming down the mountain and happened to notice two small cattle ponds only an acre or two in size. They were several hundred yards from the road, and down at the bottom of a steep slope.

I found a place to pull off the road, and climbed down to the ponds. I hadn't even bothered to bring my rod with me on the walk to the pond. As I approached the first pond, bass scattered every direction. I raced back up the hill and returned with my rod to spend a delightful afternoon catching black bass up to about 3 pounds. Since the ponds were shallow, and readily heated by the sun, it only took about 5 days of sunshine to make them fishable, even in the dead of winter. Once I went out to fish my secret ponds late in the afternoon on Christmas day. The fish were a little sluggish but I still managed to break in a new rod on a half dozen fish.

It may seem a little weird, but often times there can be excellent fishing right where you'd least expect it. Would you believe good trout fishing literally within the shadow of some of Reno's casinos? How about catching a thirty pound salmon inside the Stockton city limits? My dad even caught a 4½ pound Brown Trout within sight of a state highway, and caused a traffic jam as he carried it back to his truck. It seems that everyone is always zooming right by that particular stretch on the way to where they think the big ones bite.

Prospecting for fish in unusual places is, by its very nature, a hit and miss procedure. But then every angler is a bit of a gambler. Much like taking your chances at the casinos, if you pay your dues long enough, sooner or later you'll hit the jackpot. When prospecting for new fishing spots, remember one simple rule to the exclusion of all others, where there's water there could be fish, so give it a try. You've got nothing to lose but a little time, and you just might find that super fishing hole right under your nose.

⌘ ⌘ ⌘

GETTYSBURG ANGLING

May 1984

A few weeks ago, I was in Washington, D.C., lobbying the U.S. Congress. My flight schedule left me with a free day before I had to get on my plane at Baltimore on a Saturday night. I figured, what the heck, I could slip a pack rod into my suitcase and get in a little fishing in my spare time. The year before, I had done the same thing and had gone down into central Virginia to try my luck on pickerel and bass. The pickerel hadn't co-operated, but I'd caught a couple dozen small bass.

This time I wanted to try some eastern trout fishing but didn't know where to go. A friend in D.C. referred me to a lady who works for Trout Unlimited headquarters in the D.C. suburb of Vienna, Virginia. When I called, the lady was totally gracious, and offered to put me in touch with one of their members in the area.

The next morning a Trout Unlimited member named Bob Wesoloski, whom I had never met called and invited me to go fishing with him on his favorite trout stream up in Pennsylvania. I couldn't believe the hospitality of folks out there. Here I was, a complete stranger, and these folks were treating me as though I were some sort of visiting diplomat. Bob told me that I needn't bring any fishing gear because he'd be glad to supply me with rod, reel, flies, and any other gear I needed. All I had to bring was a pair of waders. We were going to fish a creek just outside of a little Pennsylvania town called Gettysburg.

It seemed as though I had just closed my eyes when the alarm awoke me at 4:00 on Saturday morning. My new friend Bob picked me up in his pickup, and before I realized it, we were off across Maryland heading for Pennsylvania. Since the states are so much smaller back east, a two and a half hour drive across parts of three states is about like a drive to Yosemite Park for most of us Northern Californians.

We stopped in Gettysburg for breakfast and to look at some of the endless monuments that dot the countryside. It seemed as though every farm and pasture had a statue sticking up above the grazing cows. I remarked to Bob that the darned place looked like a cemetery. Bob gave me a tolerant grin and said that it was. Sometimes I only open my mouth to change feet.

Just north of Gettysburg, we pulled off the road and parked in the bowling alley parking lot. Across the road lay a creek that ran between the farms. Conewago Creek is bordered by about a hundred yards of woods that seemed literally filled with wildflowers. The creek had been a fair trout producer until the local Trout Unlimited chapter had begun some stream improvement work with the blessing of the local landowner. Now, the holding capacity of the creek was substantially improved and the owner also received the benefit of having solved a substantial erosion problem that had been eating up his farmland.

I had brought along a couple of my trusty wooly worms from California just to see if they'd catch these sophisticated trout in Pennsylvania. Although it had rained only two days before and the creek was a little high, the water was still clear and fishable. At first I tied on some of the beaver fur nymphs that Bob supplied me with. Bob was catching fish, and I was pounding the water to a froth with little results. Upon tying on one of my weighted woollies, however, I began to catch fish, which goes to prove the theory I've long held that the best fly or lure to use is usually the one in which you have faith.

The fish were not only cooperative, they were strikingly beautiful as well. In the space of two hours I caught brooks that averaged about 12 inches, and a couple rainbows and a brown to boot. As we fished along the stream, Bob would introduce me to the anglers he knew. Although there were probably a dozen other anglers beside us on the stream, everyone was cordial and made special effort to accommodate each other.

I was also pleasantly surprised at the number of lady angler's astream. Another surprise was that almost everyone wore hip boots while fishing. In California, I had seen only one person wear hip boots in all the years I've been fishing. I guess their streams are shallower and hence hippers do the job just fine.

I really didn't mind losing all my wooly worms in both the snags and the fish, since I dug out some old streamers and even some shad flies that worked just fine. I had just finished tying on a silver and green Aztec that Carl Upton had tied when Bob inquired what the heck that monstrosity was. Just about the time he got the words out of his mouth a dandy rainbow came up and engulfed the fly. If I can get Carl to tie me a couple more of those Aztecs I'll send em' on to Bob, since I think I made a convert. Besides it'd make me feel better after having broken Bob's custom graphite rod in half.

When we finally drove away from little Conewago Creek I'm afraid that I'm the one who really got hooked. I'm hooked on the wild violets that grow everywhere, on the wild onions bigger than those in my garden, and on the turtles that sit calmly on their logs and watch you cast. I'm hooked on the contagious hospitality of my angling brethren and sistren of Trout Unlimited, and more than anything else, I'm completely and totally hooked on the bright and fiesty trout of Conewago Creek.

⌘ ⌘ ⌘

FLOATING VALLEY RIVERS

June 1985

It seems that as each year passes our daily lives get more hectic and complicated. Along with such increased pressures, it becomes increasingly important for me to find ways to relieve the pressure. Heck, we probably all need to get away from it all slow down our pace, and take the time to relax, contemplate, and recharge our batteries. I have found nothing more relaxing than float fishing our valley rivers.

There is a timeless quality about float fishing that makes it an island of sanity in a sea of urban madness. When you float around the first bend and leave our modern world behind, your companions become trees, kingfishers and beavers. Instead of the annoying sound of pagers, and cell phones, the most disruptive sounds you hear are the splash of a rising fish or the shouts of joy from kids as they leap from a cottonwood tree into their favorite swimming hole.

It's ironic that so many people are unaware of the recreational gold mine that we have right here in our back yards. We in Ripon are especially fortunate to have the Stanislaus River flow right through our town. Since the construction and filling of New Melones reservoir, the Stanislaus is undoubtedly the cleanest, most beautiful river in the valley. Although they don't have the flow that the Stanislaus has, the other valley rivers offer great float fishing as well. My favorite float trip is from McHenry Park to Mavis Stauffer Park. It's an all day trip, but the fishing is great, the scenery is beautiful, and the pressures of work are the last thing from your mind.

OK, so maybe you want to try float fishing for the first time. What do you do? That's the easy part. You can float most of the valley rivers in anything that will float, a canoe, rubber raft, car top boat, or my favorite, the canvas float tube. Fishing gear is equally an equal opportunity situation; use whichever gear you are comfortable with. Spinning gear, bait casting gear or flyrods will all produce fish for you. I was raised on a flyrod, so my first choice is to toss bass poppers, or foam rubber spiders with rubber band legs. I've also float fished with a light spinning rod, and tossed an assortment of spinners with great results. Hang a stringer off the side of your tube or boat and your fish will stay fresh all day.

What else to bring? Make sure you bring your lunch wrapped in a water tight ziplock bag, and polarized sun glasses to cut the glare, and lots of sunblock. I know it looks a little weird but I wear a light long sleeved cotton shirt when I fish. You can stick your arms in the water periodically and the evaporation will help keep you cool. The long sleeves will protect you from sunburn, bug bites, and scratches from streamside branches. A wide brimmed hat is also great. I use a John B Stetson and it protects me while keeping me cool. Always begin your float trip as early as possible because it always takes longer than you think. I remember one time putting in the water at noon and still paddling under a full moon at midnight. I had told my poor wife I'd be home by 5:00 PM and she had the sheriff's deputies out looking for me. I'll say it again – **it always takes longer than you think**.

One last piece of advice – be sure to wear your life vests. The river is a wonderful place, but it can also be dangerous. A life vest may seem like an annoyance, but its well worth it. Every week you read about drownings in the local rivers and ditches. I don't want to read about you in the obits. Float fishing is inexpensive, relaxing and a great way to fish. Heck, I just convinced myself; I'm gonna grab my gear and head for the river.

⌘ ⌘ ⌘

CHERRY CREEK ODYSSEY

April 1988

Ordinarily, I don't write precise directions to a good fishing spot. Under most circumstances, revealing a great fishing hole in print will inundate it with so many anglers that the fishing will be ruined. That won't happen in this case, however, because my secret fishing hole is so difficult to get to that almost no one is crazy enough to go back. In 35 years of fishing my favorite stretch of Cherry Creek, only one guy was ever fanatic enough to go back with me a second time. But if you are half mountain goat and half crazy, feel free to give it a try.

DISCLAIMER: the trip in and back out again is exceedingly difficult, uncomfortable, and dangerous. You will have to traverse a wet mossy cliff face above a 30 foot waterfall, you will almost certainly get poison oak, and if you get out, you will be dead tired. Don't say I didn't warn you.

Fishing should be fantastic; most years my companions and I have each averaged about 50 fish a day. The best year we ever had, I caught 106 trout while my partner caught 156 trout. Naturally, the turkey out fished me by 50 fish! That's great for one day's fishing. It's possible to get skunked, however; one year the weather was super cold, and we didn't catch a single fish. Chances are pretty good that you'll do fine. Chances are equally good that you will never see another human being astream all day.

Here goes: from Highway 120, approximately 4-5 miles East of Buck Meadows, take "Cherry Oil Road," (1N07) toward Cherry Lake. Approximately 3 miles past Early Intake, the paved road (still 1N07) crosses Cherry Creek. STOP! Before you cross the bridge, go back about 100 yards to a small dirt road going steeply **up** the hill to the right. The road immediately forks, but the left fork only goes a couple hundred yards before dead-ending at a trailhead. That trail was built by the CCC in the 1930s. It's a beautiful trail with steel cable hand rails, and even a covered bridge under a small side stream water fall. If you want to take a nice gentle mile and a quarter walk, then this is the trail for you. It goes to a Hetch Hetchy weir that is used to divert drinking water from the Cherry in drought years. Unfortunately, the fishing is lousy because the trail is so good, and everybody fishes there.

If you want great fishing take the right fork of the road which goes up the mountain for about a mile and stops. It was a construction road for the pipeline and penstock from the upper Tuolumne River that feeds the Early Intake Powerhouse. At the end of the road there is a huge talus slope from the rock generated by the construction of the tunnel. You'll see the gated entrance to the tunnel itself right there at the end of the road. Park your car at the road end and get ready to walk.

You'll want to head upstream in an easterly direction. Carefully traverse the head of the talus slope and work your way about halfway down the right hand edge. There is no trail, but slowly work your way upstream while maintaining your elevation. Walk level for about a mile and a half, still heading upstream, and the creek will be gradually rising to meet you. The last hundred yards or so you'll have to slide down a fairly steep slope to the creek. Fish upstream as far as the big waterfall and then back downstream to where you dropped in. Be careful not to go past your drop-in point, because the canyon gets awfully steep and even a helicopter can't get you out of there.

The walk out is just the reverse of the walk in – a steep climb for a hundred yards or so, staying level while angling downstream while the creek drops away, and finally there's a steep climb back up the talus slope to your car. Assuming you get out, you'll be swearing at me for the last mile or so. If you don't get out, you'll probably be swearing at me for the rest of your shortened life. But chances are you'll have had the best fishing of your life. Good luck!

⌘ ⌘ ⌘

FARM POND CRAPPIES

April 1995

As a fanatical outdoorsman I really enjoy all of the seasons. I like the blue skies and short sleeve days of summer and the long sleeve mornings and of fall. I love the sting of winter rain on my face and the silence of snow-covered woods. But I especially like springtime with its wildflowers, dogwood blossoms and great crappie fishing. While there is great crappie fishing in both the delta and the foothill reservoirs, small farmponds are best early in the season.

Because they are smaller and shallower, farmponds get warm sooner than the bigger deeper waters. All it takes is a week or so of warm spring weather, and the water will warm to the point where the crappie begin their spring feeding binge. They have been dormant all winter and make up for lost time by feeding voraciously. Sure, I fish the bigger waters too, but farmponds give me a head start on the season.

The crappie has an awfully lot going for it. They grow to a fairly large size, are extremely prolific and plentiful. Crappies are spirited fighters, and cooperative when it comes to getting hooked, and are also the best tasting fish that swims. You have to catch them before you can have a crappie feed.

One of the crappie's best features is that whatever way you like to fish, is just fine with them. Bait, spinners, and flies will all enable you to catch multitudes of crappie. Whichever method you choose, the most important thing to remember is that they are excellent predators that love to eat minnows. Since minnows congregate in the submerged brush, that's where you'll find crappie. To paraphrase an old real estate axiom, the three best places to find crappies are brush, brush, and more brush.

Obviously, if you are a bait fisher, the best bait for crappies is live minnows. Use a bobber and vary the depth of the minnow until you find the right depth. If you prefer spin fishing, your best bet is the crappie jig. Many different colors work, but my favorites are red and white, or chartreuse. As in bait fishing, vary the depth of the jig until you strike paydirt. Cast along the edge of the brush and use short jerks of the rod tip to give the jig a lively motion.

While lots of folks never thought of flyrods as a crappie weapon, I really enjoy using an ultra-light crappie jig with my flyrod for crappie. You have to slow the timing of your back cast and wait until you feel the tug of the line behind you before you start your forward cast. Otherwise, you'll spend a lot of possible fishing time in the doctor's office having hooks cut out of the back of your neck.

While I am usually an advocate of catch and release fishing so that we'll have good fishing into the future, crappie can be an exception to the rule. Crappie are just too prolific for their own good. Crappie will keep breeding until there are too many fish for the amount of food available. The result is a population of stunted fish.

Catching and eating a big batch of crappie once in awhile will actually result in a healthy population of larger fish. Don't feel guilty about keeping a big mess of farmpond crappie. Keeping a giant stringerful of crappie for a family feed is good for the fishery and it's even better on the palate.

While a fish fry is an old tradition, I really prefer to barbecue crappie and baste them with lemon butter, throw in some garlic French bread and a good white wine, and you've got a meal fit for a king. Well, there you have it. Grab your rod, head for your local farmpond and some sunshine, great fun, and some of the finest tasting fish in the world, the crappie.

⌘ ⌘ ⌘

THE MONSTER TROUT OF PYRAMID LAKE

February 2005

A couple times I have mentioned places in California to catch really large trout. Unfortunately, most of them require walking or rappelling into impossible places. That's sort of the nature of catching really big fish—if it was easy, everybody would do it. Like everything else in life, there is an exception to almost every rule. The exception to the "giant trout are impossible to catch" rule, where you stand a really good chance of catching a trout over 8 pounds, is a place called Pyramid Lake that lies just Northeast of Reno, Nevada. Located on the huge Paiute Indian Reservation, Pyramid Lake is populated by Lahontan Cutthroat Trout which can grow to over 40 pounds.

I kid you not! On a late winter day at Pyramid, five pound cutthroat trout are fairly common and the biggest fish in any given day will usually be over 10 pounds. Think about that, five to ten pound trout! Really! You've heard the old adage that if it seems too good to be true, it usually is. Well, that's not the case with Pyramid Lake. The average angler really does stand a pretty good chance of catching a huge trout at Pyramid.

The most productive method of catching Pyramid Cutts is fly fishing by wading out from shore as far as possible and casting big woolly worms or wooly buggers on a fast sinking line. Many anglers take a milk crate or a short step ladder out into waist deep water to serve as a casting platform. You cast as far out into the lake as you can, wait a minute or so to let your line settle to the bottom, and then strip your line back toward you in short pulls.

Insulated neoprene waders are a must as are long johns underneath and neoprene gloves to keep your fingers from freezing. It's great to bring along an RV to get warm in. About the longest I can stand the cold at one time is a half hour, so I come back to the RV and stick my hands in a cup of boiling coffee to thaw them.

You must buy a special tribal fishing license, and you don't need a Nevada license as long as you only fish on Pyramid Lake. There are great hotel accommodations in the Reno-Sparks area and after a hard day's fishing you can enjoy all of the amenities that go along with the area. The fishing regulations are fairly complicated because of some unusual size limits. Check with the Tribal authorities at Sutcliff where you get your license. Actually, I would recommend you take lots of photos and release everything. That's how you keep a great fishery.

If you want to make it easy on yourself, hire a local guide to show you the ropes. I contacted Mario Walther of the Reno Flyshop at 775-825-3474 and had a delightful chat, They will guide you and a buddy for a full day for $350 and teach you everything you need to know. Mario estimates that you'll catch bunches of really large trout. Some of their anglers have caught and released trout over 10 pounds! If you want a trout to hang on the wall, you can now take several photos and a few simple measurements and your taxidermist can make a beautiful mounted trout for your wall. Even better still, your trophy trout gets released to spawn and pass on his wonderful genes! How's that for a happy ending?

⌘ ⌘ ⌘

FLYROD BASS

August 2009

For the past 19 years I've lived about 300 yards from the Stanislaus River as it flows through Ripon. In fact, I moved there because of the river and the great flyfishing for bass there. It's about a 5 minute walk from my front door to being knee-deep in the river. Unfortunately, I don't spend nearly enough time fishing. Work seems to get in the way. Clearly, I have to readjust my priorities. I first got hooked on flyfishing as a child by my dad. We fished at least one day out of almost every weekend in the Sierra Nevada Mountains. I literally cannot remember when I began flyfishing for trout. In fact, until I was about 12, I pretty much thought that flyfishing was the only way people fished for trout.

I also fished for bass, panfish and catfish. As small children, my dad would take my brother, sister and me out to one of the Islands in the San Joaquin Delta along with a big supply of worms and live minnows. For a kid there's nothing quite like seeing that bobber begin to twitch, and then race around in small circles, just before your quarry gets serious and jerks that bobber completely under in what seems like a mad dash for the ocean!

Although catching a washtub full of bluegills, crappie, and catfish was the usual result of our Delta excursions, occasionally, we'd get a largemouth bass as an added bonus. I guess that reinforced the idea that bass were caught using bait or spinning gear. It simply never occurred to me that you could fish for bass with a flyrod.

There was no blinding epiphany where a bolt of lightning, or a parting of the Heavens revealed flyfishing for bass to me. Along about the middle 1970's I accidentally stumbled across catching bass with a flyrod. In looking back, my fly-rodding for bass was a sort of gradual conversion that probably began on the Merced River downstream from Yosemite Park.

There are some really nice trout in the lower Merced with big pools connected by rocky riffles. In the El Portal stretch of the Merced, the water gets pretty warm in summer, and occasionally my fly would get slammed, and my rod almost jerked from my hand, following which a glistening smallmouth bass would leap into the sunlight trying to rid himself of my fly. I'd yell with delight until I realized that it was just a darned old bass fouling up my trout fishing.

Slowly it began to dawn on me that maybe these bass weren't simply a distraction from my beloved trout, but a darned good game fish that deserved more attention. I began to check out books on bass fishing at the local library and found that some people actually fished for bass with a fly on purpose. The local flyfishing club was also helpful and had several guys who tied flies specifically designed to catch bass.

Bass flies are quite different from the trout flies I was used to tying. They are almost always larger than trout flies, which is good for beginning fly tiers because big flies are easier to tie than microscopic trout flies. Many bass flies are tied with deer hair which is hollow and floats extremely well. It takes some practice to learn to spin deer hair around a hook, but once you figure it out, your flies become almost unsinkable.

As you progress in your metamorphosis of becoming a bass flyrodder you learn that smallmouth bass prefer moving rocky water at temperatures warmer than those preferred by trout, but cooler than that preferred by largemouth bass.

By contrast, largemouth prefers warmer, slower moving water and sandy or clay bottoms. In essence, smallmouth are stream dwellers and largemouth are lake dwellers. Of course there are exceptions to every rule, but if you fish the rivers on the valley floor, you'll almost always find the largemouth in the slower waters and the smallmouth in the swifter runs. Fish rocky or rip-rapped stretches for smallmouth and quieter back eddies with overhead cover for largemouth.

Why fish for bass with a flyrod at all? The answer is excitement. Clearly, the most productive methods are bait and spinning gear. A fly rod, by definition, is a longer rod that bends easily and uses lighter lines. I heard a presentation the other day by a former bass pro who says he regularly uses 80 pound test line with his bait-casting bass rig.

I think that the heaviest fly leader I've ever used in my life was 15 pound test. In flyfishing, the rod does the work of subduing the fish instead of the line. When you have a large bass slam into one of your hand tied bass flies for the first time, it will be you who gets hooked, not the bass. The strike of a big bass is so savage that it will make your heart race and you'll think you've hooked into a 100 pound ocean dweller that got into your river by mistake. Believe me, if you hook a 5 pound bass on a flyrod, not only will your butt pucker, but you'll be a flyrod bass fisher forever more. Don't take my word for it – get out there and try flyrodding for bass!

⌘ ⌘ ⌘

SKI RESORT FISHING

October 2009

Almost exactly 100 years ago, my grandfather earned a living trout fishing. He would fish the Gunnison River in Colorado and sell his fish to the mining and logging camps in nearby Crested Butte. In the mid 1980s I found myself fishing in some of the same streams grandpa had fished in 1905. Where Crested Butte was once a mining and logging town, it's now a ski resort and tourist Mecca complete with condos, tennis courts and gourmet restaurants. I'm a little slow when it comes to learning new stuff, and it probably took me 20 years to figure out that ski resorts are almost always great places to fish as well as ski. In addition to Crested Butte, I discovered that there is great fishing around the Mammouth Lakes Ski Resort in California as well as near the ski chalets of Park City, Utah. I've heard there's equally good fishing if you're based in Jackson Hole, Wyoming or Sun Valley, Idaho.

Why would any ordinary angler want to hang out where there are antique shops and fancy eateries populated by movie stars and aging hippies driving Volvos? When you stop and think about it, there is actually quite a bit of logic is using a ski resort as your angling H.Q. Foremost, of course, is that ski resorts are located high in the mountains at least somewhat removed from civilization, and secondly, many of those yuppie eateries actually put out some first-class food. A really neat advantage of ski resort angling is that lodging is quite affordable in the off-ski season. Mammouth Lakes, for example, has a huge population in winter and shrinks by about 70% in mid summer. A 5 bedroom chalet in Park City that rents for $2,000 a night (no kidding!) is only $500 a night in the off season. This weekend, 4 of my high school buddies and I along with our wives, are heading to Park City for a little fishing, golf, card playing, shopping, and other forms of R and R. Our lodging bill per head will be about the same cost as a weekend in Modesto. Another advantage of ski resort angling is the plethora of fly shops and guide services. When the ski season ends, the residents there have to keep on buying groceries and paying their mortgages. Many of the ski shops do a spring conversion that's like magic. One day it's a ski shop run by a guy named Helmut, and ALAKA-ZAM, the next day it's a fly shop run by a guy named Hank. The local shops are often complete with guided float trips on the nearby streams, equipment rentals and a great selection of hand tied flies. Actually many of those guides really are knowledgeable about local waters and conditions.

If it's your first time angling in a ski area, I heartily recommend visiting the local shop and booking at least a half day float trip. You'll learn all kinds of useful techniques and area hot spots, as well as tips on staying out of trouble. Pretty much everybody knows not to mess with bear cubs, since mama bears are fiercely protective of their young. It never occurred to me, however, that a mama moose will stomp you just as dead as if you'd been mauled by a bear. Moose? Yep, they're out there, and you have to pay attention if you want to come home in one piece.

As much as I delight in sitting around the campfire swapping lies and watching stars, there are real advantages to coming back from a hard days fishing, taking a hot shower, eating a gourmet meal, and unwinding in a hot tub. Quite truthfully, of my 4 buddies and me, none of our wives is really a serious angler. But in a major ski resort, there's usually some great shopping nearby and while we guys are off getting sunburned and bug-bit, our spouses are off in search of the ideal bargain. Ski resort angling definitely promotes marital harmony.

What the heck, throw a dart at a map of the West, locate the nearest good sized ski resort, and give it a try. You might just have a great time.

⌘ ⌘ ⌘

WOMEN ANGLERS

February 2010

It must have been 30 years ago that I was fishing on the opening day of trout season with a couple buddies. As is often the case, there were still patches of snow on the ground and the streams were running high and cold. Flyfishing under such conditions was going to be pretty tough because if the fish can't see your fly, you can't catch them. One of the guys spoke up in a whispered voice: "Hey, look! There's a girl fishing that flooded meadow."

Sure enough, a young woman in her early 20s was casting a fly in the knee deep water of a flooded meadow. Back then, you didn't ordinarily see a lot of women trout fishing in the Sierras, so we all stopped to watch the rare sight. The first thing that struck me was that this angler was fishing in exactly the right spot.

Most of the stream was raging white water but the flooded meadow allowed the water to spread out and calm down to a less frantic speed. When a stream floods a meadow there are thousands of ants, beetles, worms, and other delicious critters caught up in the rising waters. The flooded meadow was not only a refuge for trout, but a regular feast as well. This girl was fishing the most productive spot imaginable.

On closer inspection, something else caught my eye; the angler was casting a bright, flashy fly called a Royal Coachman, which was not only easier for the angler to see, but easily spotted by the trout as well. We watched, transfixed, as the lady angler carefully worked her fly, cast after cast, among the willow clumps in the flooded meadow.

As we watched, a dark shape dashed out of the willows and smashed the fly. The rod was bent and the angler hooked into a nice Brown Trout that looked to be about 14 to 15 inches. We were watching a very skilled angler at work. One of my buddies shook his head and said, "Yo, Don. That's gotta be your kind of girl!"

As the years have passed, flyfishing has gained in popularity but the number of women anglers has grown geometrically as well. Ordinarily a lot of folks perceive fishing as a man's sport, and 50 years ago it probably was. But as they say, "the times, they are a changing," and now it's not uncommon at all to see women out in the streams right along with the men.

Over the years I have taught numerous novices the basics of flyfishing. I have found that women unequivocally make better angling students than men. Flyfishing is much more dependent upon timing than upon brute strength. Men will undoubtedly try to force that fly out there rather than use finesse. Women adjust more readily to the rhythm of the rod than men do.

In addition to fishing, women numbers are exploding in almost all outdoor pursuits, from camping, to backpacking, to snowshoeing. In fact one of my old schoolmates, Cathy Anderson-Meyers, is an outdoor instructor for the famous REI chain. Cathy teaches, snowshoeing, mountain, biking and a host of other outdoor sports. I don't know about anyone else, but I welcome my women angler friends. Fishing can be enjoyed by anyone, and it's high time that women can join.

⌘ ⌘ ⌘

Don't Forget Your Camera!

FISHING WITH KIDS

March 1984

I took my daughter Julie fishing with me last Sunday. Before we left, I called one of my friends to get permission to fish in his farm pond. Then we stopped at the local bait shop for minnows and headed out. Ordinarily, I prefer to fish farm ponds with either a fly rod or with spinning gear. With a kid along, however, it's a different story. Kids almost universally do better if they have a big bobber to watch, and this trip was no exception.

We hadn't been at the pond more than 10 minutes before Julie's bobber began to behave strangely, circling frantically as though something was terrifying the hapless minnow. Sure enough, after a few minutes, the big red and white bobber began to bob vigorously. After losing a few minnows to impatience, Julie managed to land a tremendous bass of nine inches long.

If there's anything absolutely mandatory for keeping a kid entranced while fishing, it's having consistent action. I recall going fishing when I was young with my brother, sister and my beleaguered dad. We'd go out to a sleepy backwater in the Delta, armed with simple closed-faced reels, short rods, and a seemingly endless supply of worms. It always seemed as if poor dad spent most of his time putting worms on hooks, untangling lines, and unhooking bluegills. When we got a galvanized washtub filled with bluegills, catfish and an occasional dumb bass, we'd rush for home to release our fish in our backyard wading pool.

Another surefire way to keep kids' appetite whetted for fishing excursions is to bring along about twice as much food as you think you'll need. It's amazing how many apples, oranges, and assorted candy kids can consume when they're fishing. Prior to our childhood fishing excursions, we always stopped by dad's drug store and raided the candy section. Big Hunks, Abba Zabbas, Corn Nuts, and M and Ms were always at the top of our list. Other staples that were a big hit were the enough assorted sodas to fill an ice chest. It's hard to go wrong with black cherry, crème soda, lemon-lime, and orange flavored sodas.

Julie had a ball catching minnows out of the minnow bucket, throwing pebbles in the pond, and watching the fish we'd caught swimming around in our water-filled ice chest. Another great way to keep kids interested and wanting to come back again, is to quit early, before they have a chance to get bored. We had caught four small bass and one large one that broke off right next to shore. What's fishing trip without the big one that got away?

On almost every trip, there's bound to be at least one thing you'll forget. While you can get by without some items, take special care to always bring your camera. Kids grow up so fast, the last thing you want to forget is your camera. The photos you take out fishing with kids will become priceless. In a few years those photos will become your most prized possessions. Don't forget your camera!

One final bit of advice when taking kids fishing is to take it easy on them. Don't try having them make strenuous hikes until they're old enough to handle it. Take your little ones to easy places at first to get them hooked on fishing. Once they're old enough to become incurably addicted, you can psych them up for the longer trips.

Observe the above simple guidelines and you'll have a lifetime fishing partner. I knew an old codger who tried those tricks on me, and I'm still bugging him to go fishing 30 years later. Give it a try and you'll never regret it.

⌘ ⌘ ⌘

Section Five

GEAR AND TECHNIQUES

THE UGLY DUCKLING

January 1984

A friend once asked me how long I had been flyfishing. I explained that while I probably wasn't born with a flyrod, I honestly couldn't remember not having fished with one. I grew up thinking that everyone fished with the same long rod as me. Since I grew up in the valley, trout fishing was only reachable by car and unreachable to the town's kids on our bicycles.

Our secret fishing hole was Black Lake, a small pond about 3 or 4 miles out of town just past the city sewer ponds. It must not have been too much of a secret, since at least half the kids in town rode their bikes out there to fish. Over time, I began to notice that my rod was a lot longer than that of any of the other kids. To make matters worse, my darned old long rod had a funny reel and wouldn't cast a bobber and a worm worth a darn.

I began to feel like the ugly duckling, all the other kids could cast their bobber's way out in the middle of the lake and all I could reach was the sunken trees right next to the shore. It never dawned on me that the other guys never caught any fish out there in the middle, but that they caught their fish right next to the brush just like I did. We caught bluegills, crappie, baby stripers and once in awhile some lucky stiff would catch a bass. I don't think I ever did catch a bass with that stupid long rod.

One day I was fishing next to shore as always when I got a hefty bite. I reared back to set the hook and suddenly, the battle was on. I was in seventh heaven, and kids began to come from all around the lake to see what kind of monster "old long rod" had caught. When I finally brought the monster to shore, I had no idea what kind of fish this long, ugly, creature was. Everybody looked at everybody else, and no one knew the answer.

Finally someone called Jim Corso over to take a look. Everyone knew that Jim knew just everything about fishing. Jim was amazed. "That's a sturgeon," he exclaimed, "My dad caught one before. That's great, Don!" proclaimed Jim, "nobody ever caught a sturgeon at Black Lake before." My monster sturgeon must have been every bit of two feet long.

I was basking in the glory of my piscatorial prowess when suddenly old Jim (he was twelve), noticed my funny long rod. He asked if he could look at it, then examined it slowly. "This is a fly rod isn't it?" he inquired. "Well, yeah, it is," I replied somewhat hesitantly. "No kidding, I sure wish I had a fly rod."

Suddenly, every guy on the lake wanted to borrow my fly rod so they could catch a sturgeon too. One guy even offered to trade me his bike for it. Son of a gun if my old ugly duckling fly rod hadn't turned into a swan. I turned down all offers to part with my long rod and peddled home on my bike with my monster two foot sturgeon prominently displayed in my basket. Yes, indeed, maybe those long fly rods weren't so bad after all.

⌘ ⌘ ⌘

FACETS OF A KNIFE

June 1985

It began years ago when my parents gave me a hand-made silver pocket knife for my birthday. It was engraved "From Mother and Dad" on one side and engraved on the other side was my name and the date. That knife was and still is a work of art, the same custom knife maker had made similar knives for Bob Hope, Bing Crosby, and a couple of governors.

More important than the beauty of my new knife, was its utility. Although the sides were silver the blades were forged from no-nonsense spring steel. Naturally, because of the engraving, my knife held great sentimental value too. I guess because I treasured it so much I bought my dad an engraved knife a few years later for his birthday. Soon a tradition had developed and over the years we have given each other engraved knives for birthdays, Christmas, and any other occasion we can justify.

I think that fascination with a fine cutting instrument is something that almost universal. Doesn't everyone enjoy the feel of a fine knife in their hand? Oh sure, I love the feel of casting a classic bamboo flyrod, or the silky smoothness of walnut gunstock, but it can't compare to the heft of a masterfully built knife.

Several years ago I was lucky enough to get tickets to see the King Tut exhibit when it was touring the world. Lo and behold! There was an incredibly beautiful gold inlaid knife among the exhibits. From that point I felt a kinship with a boy king who died thousands of years ago.

Not only can knives have sentimental value, or be works of art, but they are supremely utilitarian. Every outdoor enthusiast from mountain to jungle owns at least one knife. Not only outdoor fanatics carry knives but probably millions of pocket knives are carried every day in the modern jungles we call cities.

When I was growing up, a knife was a tool that you always carried with you, even at school. No one thought anything unusual about it at all. I remember showing one of my knives at school to my debate teacher Ernie Poletti and him showing me his knife in return. Boy how times have changed! I regularly remind my son, Bo, to be careful never to take his knife to school because it's almost sure grounds for punishment.

I know that the schools have no choice but to ban knives, but still, it seems a shame that our society now views an incredibly handy tool as a weapon instead. Wouldn't it be nice if we could once again view a knife as a tool that most responsible people wouldn't be without? I guess that's the key "responsible people."

The Boy Scouts have the right idea. In scouting, toting a knife is a privilege that must be earned by the older boys by studying knife safety and passing an exam. It is also a privilege that can be revoked if they ever violate any of the safety rules.

Carrying a good sharp knife can save your life. I just read how a small boat off the coast of Alaska got its anchor rope fouled in the tail flukes of a 40 ton humpback whale. Only quick work with a handy knife prevented the whale from accidentally sinking the boat. While that must have been a pretty exciting few minutes, chances are you won't need your knife to save your life. But you never know, do you?

One of my fishing buddies was fishing along the Stanislaus near Knights Ferry when his dog got bitten by a large rattler. Bob quickly whipped out his knife and shaved the dog's hair from the bite area so he could apply the suction device necessary to suck out the poison. After a couple days at the vet the dog was fine. But the vet told us that if Bob hadn't been able to quickly shave the bite area and get the poison sucked out, his dog would have surely died.

Nothing is more important in regard to a knife than keeping it really sharp. You may not believe the old adage, that you are more likely to cut yourself with a dull knife than with a sharp one, but it's true. How can that be? Easy, with a dull knife you press harder, then the knife invariably slips and whack, you've slashed yourself!

Keep your knife sharp and it'll save you a lot of grief. Use a stone that has at least two sharpening surfaces, a course side and a fine side. Begin on the course side and proceed to the finer side. Then hone the knife with a sharpening steel, or a ceramic rod. Finally, for a razor sharp edge, strop your knife on a leather razor strop. When you're done you should be able to shave with your knife. I have literally shaved off a two year old beard with my pocket knife. I didn't knick myself, and when I was done my face was smooth as a baby's bottom.

While the Boy Scouts have developed some great safety rules such as always closing a pocket knife before passing it to anyone, I have developed a more stringent one of my own, I've developed a habit of never, ever loaning my knife to anyone. If someone asks to use my knife, I simply ask what they need cut and then cut it for them. That way, I know my knife won't get used as a screwdriver, paint can opener, or put to similar obscene uses. My knife is always ready to skin a critter, cut a rope or shave a snake bite, but I'll be damned if I'm going to let some idiot use it to open cans.

If you're ever stuck for a gift idea for a friend who is an outdoor enthusiast, you can always get him a knife. Even if he already has a dozen of them, he can always use another knife.

⌘ ⌘ ⌘

DRY FLIES, WET FLIES

May 1986

For the last 150 years or so, a debate has taken place among fly fishers over the merits of dry flies versus wet flies. Prior to about 1850, metal technology was not sophisticated enough to produce a hook that was both strong and light. As hooks became stronger and lighter, anglers discovered that by using just the right materials, and by whipping the fly rapidly thru the air to dry it out before each cast, you could get a fly to float on the waters surface. If you floated a fly just right over a feeding fish, you could con the fish into rising to the surface and taking your fly.

Dry fly fishing, as the new technique was known, became the goal that sophisticated anglers strove to achieve. Nothing could be more satisfying than tricking a trout to the surface to take your fly. I've gotta admit that making a picture perfect cast and having a trout take it from the surface of a calm trout stream is pretty cool. In my mind's eye I can picture just such an occasion where it all came together. I spotted a rising trout taking insects from the surface. I tied on a Royal Coachman, and carefully made a perfect cast. The trout rose and took the fly in a picture perfect moment, and I landed a nice brown trout about 14 inches long.

Wet fly fishing, in addition to having been around since the time of Alexander the Great, consists of trying to imitate insects and other trout foods that are below the surface of the water. A really great book on the subject is "Larger Trout for the Western Flyfisher" by Charlie Brooks. In his book, Brooks observes that trout do 90% of their feeding **under** the water and only 10% on the surface. Hence, Brooks believes that your chances of catching fish are about 10 times greater if you're fishing with a sunken fly. OK, now we've got the basic idea—dry flies are fished on the waters surface, and wet flies are fished below the surface. Essentially, there are two major methods in dry fly fishing. One is called "Matching the Hatch," in which you try to imitate a fly which the trout are taking on the surface at any given time.

Many books have been written on imitating the exact insect that is hatching at the time by selecting just the right fly from your fly box or by whipping out your fly tying kit and tying a duplicate to the bug hatching in front of you. Fly tiers go to great lengths to match the hatch.

They sometimes have special nets to capture the bugs, magnifying glasses to study them and streamside identification books to identify precisely which bug it is. They take classes in aquatic entomology and learn all the Latin names of the bugs they will learn to imitate. When a hatch occurs on a warm spring morning, a dedicated dry fly angler can ID the bug as an *Ephemerella Ephemoptera* or as a *Pteronarcys Californica*. We ordinary mortals would look at the above critters and see either a Mayfly or a Stonefly.

The other method of dry fly angling is to try and create an artificial hatch by floating the same fly over the same fish time after time until the trout is fooled into thinking an insect hatch is happening. The artificial hatch method takes determination and patience. You've got to persist in making the exact same cast with the exact same fly for as long as it takes to convince that one fish that he's hungry. Once again the challenge is great and so is the mental reward when you finally fool your quarry.

Wet fly fishing can also be divided into two schools of thought: the Imitators and the Attractors. Imitators are trying to create and cast flies that resemble specific bugs. In the early stages of an aquatic bug's life, they are called nymphs which are the little critters crawl along the bottom of a stream hoping not to be washed away by the current or eaten by prowling trout. Nymphs live for a year or two on the stream bottom before they change (much like caterpillars turning into butterflies) into emergers which then swim to the surface, and finally hatch into adults who then fly away to breed and continue their species.

The wet fly angler of the Imitation School seeks to copy either the nymphs or the emergers which trout love to devour. The anglers belonging to the attractor school use flies that don't really imitate a specific bug, but that are just "buggy" looking in general. The Wooly Worm and the Matuka don't really resemble any bug at all, but are among the most effective of all wet flies. If you can stand the cold, bouncing a Wooly Worm along the bottom of Pyramid Lake is probably your best chance in this life to catch a trout over 10 pounds.

Now you've got the basics of the dry fly/ wet fly theories under your belt. Which is better? Which ever one you prefer, of course. If you want the challenge of tying exactly the right fly and making the perfect cast to outwit a crafty old trout, then dry fly fishing should be just what you like. If you enjoy exploring more water and having your rod slammed almost out of your hand, then maybe wet fly fishing is for you. Whichever you choose, you can't go wrong—just get out there and go fishing.

⌘ ⌘ ⌘

THE FISHING LOG

May 1987

Since I couldn't get away to go fishing last weekend, I did the next best thing, I drug out my old fishing logs and began to relive fishing trips from years past. Actually, reliving old fishing trips is only one of many great reasons to keep your own fishing log. Recording stream conditions, weather patterns, and flies, lures, baits and techniques used can help improve your fishing. Jotting down unusual wildlife you spot, or interesting rock and mineral formations, notes on mining ruins, or Indian artifacts can help increase your enjoyment of your outdoor excursions. Who knows, maybe I'll go back to that molybdenum deposit I found in the Stanislaus National Forest and stake out a mining claim.

A ritual I observe each year is to go through the previous year's fishing log and tally up the years fishing results. I count all the days I fished, how many fish I caught, how many I released, my average catch per day, what species were caught, how many different streams I've fished, etc.

Sometimes it's troublesome to write all the information down, but it pays good dividends over the long haul. I used to be especially proud of how many fish I caught, but as years went by I was more concerned with how big the fish were, and eventually I became more concerned with how many species I could catch and identify.

1973 was a banner year for total number of fish. I caught 824 trout in 29 days on the water for an average of 28.41 fish per day. Ten years later in 1983, I only fished a total a total of 14 days but the size of the fish was much larger, and I was releasing more fish unharmed. In 1993 I was with my 7 year old daughter and 5 year old son drowning minnows below a bobber in a farm pond.

Now, I'm placing more emphasis on interesting events, like the time I floated sideways down the creek in my car, or the thunderstorm that terrified my dog so that I had to carry her under one arm while I tried to fish one handed. In September of 1976 I caught two fish at once, a smallmouth bass on my top fly and a rainbow trout on my bottom fly!

I heartily recommend that you keep an angling log to record your fishing progress, as well as to preserve the memories that you'll savor in later years. As you read them, you'll relive those great days when everything went perfect, and laugh at those days when you couldn't do anything right. The images of angling buddies long since passed on will come to mind, and you'll smile at the memory.

You can become a better angler by studying your old logs to find out what techniques work under certain conditions, and which do not. When you face similar conditions, you'll have a head start. I record water temperature, air temperature, altitude, water clarity, cloud cover, flies used, precipitation, and which flies caught fish. I have designed my own form and included sections for fish caught (by species), line and leader used, starting and ending time and then a section for general notes.

I try to always try to take a long lunch break on the stream, not only to eat, but to make log entries, and sometimes even just take a nap on a sunny sand bar. I've never taken my blood pressure while I'm fishing, but I'd be willing to bet it drops substantially the minute I step into the stream.

Try an angling log this year. It's simple, free, usually improves your fishing, and sure as the dickens increases the enjoyment you get out of fishing. What the heck, give it a try!

⌘ ⌘ ⌘

ROADKILL TREASURES

October 2007

A couple months ago, I was driving along a country road when the car ahead of me slammed on his brakes and came to a dead stop in the middle of the road. The guy jumped out and ran out in front of his car. I figured there was either a terrible accident, or I had encountered another fly tier stopping to harvest a road kill treasure. Sure enough, as I pulled around the guy he had his jackknife out and was removing the tail from a road killed raccoon. At this point you might ask yourself, "What kind of a nutcase stops to salvage road killed animals?" Fly tiers, that's who.

Fly tying is an avocation that dates back to at least the ancient Greeks. Somewhere back in the dim mists of time, some ancient angler discovered that you could tie some bits of fur or feather around a hook and actually catch fish with it. The art of fly tying has advanced to the point where it seems as if when you drop some of today's modern flies in the water, they might swim away. Not only is fly tying an effective way of catching fish, but it's also a most rewarding hobby.

Probably the first reason that comes to mind for tying your own, at least at first, is the satisfaction you can get from catching a trout, bass, or whatever, on a fly that you made with your own hands. A couple decades ago, I belonged to Big Brothers of America, and had a youngster named Billy that I drug out into the woods and streams with me on a pretty regular basis. In all the times we spent together, I never saw Billy more thrilled than when he caught his first trout on a fly he tied all by himself. It was a wretched excuse for a fly that no self respecting fish would bite, but somehow

Billy found a demented six inch trout dumb enough to hit it. Nothing excited him more than catching that little fish, not even the new 22 he got for Christmas. Another more practical reason for tying your own flies is cost. Store bought trout flies can often cost between $1.00 and $2.50 each, while bass flies and saltwater flies are even higher. Once you've lost a couple dozen flies, on rocks or in trees or big fish, you begin to think there has to be a cheaper way. If you tie your own, you can sit down in front of a warm fire on a winter night and turn out flies that cost you less than a quarter each. Heck, that kind of savings could even pay for your brandy.

Perhaps the best reason of all is that you can tie exactly what you want instead of having to buy a fly that's "close enough." A perfect case in point is the wooly worm fly that my friends give me such a hard time over. Dry flies are supposed to float in the surface film on top of the water, and probably 90% of all flies sold are dry flies. Wet flies, on the other hand, sink below the surface where the fish are. I prefer wet flies. But most woolly worms you find in stores are made from materials especially selected to float.

There are actually chicken breeders who raise birds exclusively for sale to fly tiers. A top grade dry fly chicken hide will sell for over $100. It's hard to believe that a dead chicken could cost over $100. I, however, buy a common barnyard variety Plymouth Rock chicken skin for less than $10, because it's soft webby feathers absorb water and sink instead of float. Because I tie my own, I get what I want even if it isn't politically correct.

Another example of the benefits of tying your own is when you're out on the stream and the fish decide to get really picky and only take one particular kind of fly. You haven't got it in your fly vest and the local tackle shop is sold out. What do you do? If you are a fly tier, you whip out your trusty tying kit and tie up a couple of the hot flies that will knock em dead. Of course, it is possible to get carried away with the streamside "match the hatch" routine. Several years ago, two buddies from Modesto and I drove up to Beaver Creek for a day's fishing and discovered a tremendous hatch of flying ants.

Those flying ants were everywhere, and the trout were whipping the water into a froth gorging on them. I tied on a woolly worm and headed downstream, Bob tied on a Royal Wulf dry fly and headed upstream while Bud sat down to his fly vise and began to tie ant imitations. A couple hours later we met back at the car and found out how well we'd done. Bob had caught and released over 30 trout before he broke his rod tip and had to quit, I had caught over 50 trout, and Bud had 6 fish and several dozen of the prettiest ant flies you'd ever want to see.

A side benefit to tying your own is that it can help keep you from going mad with cabin fever when you might otherwise be climbing the walls. It's not quite as good as going fishing, but getting out the vise and feathers on a rainy night and whipping up a few flies for the coming season is pretty therapeutic.

Once you get a little basic instruction, fly tying is really quite easy. If I can do it, almost anybody can. If you think you'd like to try your hand at fly tying, drop me a line at don.moyer@gmail.com, and I'll put you in touch with the local fly club who'd love to expose you to their wonderful and addicting sport.

⌘ ⌘ ⌘

THE CARCANO

November 2008

The year 1961 was a kinder, gentler time. Our nation shifted from worrying about Ike's golf score to wondering who had made John Kennedy's rocking chair. American auto makers reigned supreme, and General Motors had just introduced its revolutionary new rear wheel drive car that provided both sports car like handling and fuel economy, the Corvair.

Sportsmen too had it pretty good. The daily trout limit was 25 fish, you could buy two deer tags and a bear tag each year, and a young man was able to get his big game tags when he reached his 12th birthday. I recall it well because I had gotten my first 22 rifle and my first 12 gauge shotgun the year before. I could hunt small game like rabbits and squirrels as well as ducks, pheasants and quail. My hunting universe was almost complete. The only thing I needed was a real honest to goodness big bore rifle with which to hunt big game like deer and bear.

Much like Ralphie in "A Christmas Story," I kept dropping hints to my parents that a real big game rifle would be greatly appreciated. Unlike Ralphie, however, my parents never seemed to get the hint. I think my mother was worried I'd get eaten by a bear.

Like most other kids at the time, I was a regular reader of the big 3 outdoor magazines: *Outdoor Life*, *Field and Stream*, and *Sports Afield*. They were full of great stories, how-to articles, and ads which promised products guaranteed to improve your fishing and hunting. I regularly sent off for every free catalog available. One of the best catalogs (besides Herters of Waseca, Minnesota) was the catalog from P and

S Sales of Tulsa, Oklahoma. P and S was a military surplus store that had amazing bargains you just couldn't find elsewhere. They had horse blanket pins, surplus navy watch caps, hand cranked generators for field phones, and even McClelland saddles left over from the Civil War.

Just as Ralphie dreamed of his Red Ryder BB gun, I perused the pages of my catalogues looking for an affordable big game rifle. One day like a bolt from the blue, there it was! An advertisement for a special buy on surplus military rifles from Italy. I could buy my very own deer and bear rifle for only $12.95 plus shipping and handling.

There, in a fuzzy black and white illustration, was the answer to my prayers, a 6.5 millimeter Italian Carcano with folding bayonet. Not wanting to bother my Mom and Dad with such a trivial matter, I bought a postal money order with my paper route money and arranged to have my new treasure shipped to my buddy Ray's house. Naturally, when a surplus rifle arrived at Ray's, his parents called my parents and the vigaro hit the Mixmaster.

Eventually, my Dad forgave me, and we went out to the range to test my new prize. Unfortunately, the old maxim of "you get what you pay for" kicked in. My new gun had a tendency to "keyhole." If you are unfamiliar with the term, keyholing is when a bullet tumbles end over end in flight. When a gun keyholes, the path of the bullet is extremely erratic and any kind of accuracy is impossible. I had spent my hard earned paper route money on a piece of junk!

Sometime later, Dad helped me select a fine surplus Mauser in 7mm that is still a great shooting gun today. The old 6.5mm Italian Carcano with folding bayonet was stuck in the back of the closet for years and lost in the mists of time. A few years after that, a deranged nutcase named Lee Harvey Oswald bought an almost identical rifle by mail order and had it shipped to a phony P.O.Box in Dallas.

Last fall, I was sitting around a reunion of old high school buddies just reminiscing about the good old days when Ray brought up how I'd gotten him in trouble by having a rifle shipped to his address. Somehow, I'm always the one who gets blamed for getting everybody else in trouble. I tell my kids not to believe those lies.

All of a sudden, right in the middle of Ray's lie, old Dave chimes in with, "Hey, I've got that gun in my closet!" It turns out that I had given it to my brother who tried to shoot it and gave up and who then sold it to Dave who got the same results. It was still a piece of junk. Just for old time's sake, I offered to buy the old Carcano from Dave, who graciously gave it to me. Thanks, Dave, I owe you one.

Getting that old 6.5 mm carbine back was like being reunited with an old friend. I recall that the first time I fired it, I tied a cord to the trigger and covered the action with sandbags just in case it exploded. It did fire, but the keyhole effect is a fatal flaw in a gun. It would never be anything more than an interesting curio to hang on a wall.

This time, however, I did a little research on the Web and determined from the markings cast in the steel that mine was a cavalry model carbine that was made in the city of Gardone in northern Italy in 1940. Gardone has been known for its numerous gun makers since the 1500s and Beretta Arms still has its world headquarters there today. Unfortunately, it was almost certainly not made by Beretta because they made only custom guns for Mussolini's private security force and similar custom work. Still, just picking up my old Carcano brings back memories of a simpler time when our nation was successful and prosperous. If only I could just get my buddies to stop telling those tall tales about me getting them in trouble.

⌘ ⌘ ⌘

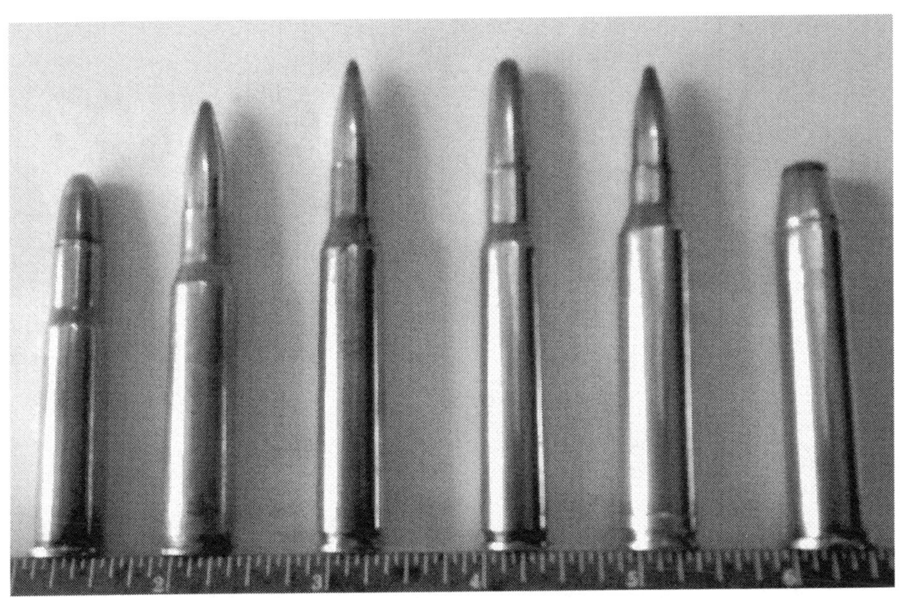

30-30 7x57 mm 270 Win 30-06 7 mm Mag 45-70

Some of the More Popular Rifle Cartridges

THE WORLD'S BEST CARTRIDGE

November 2009

Trying to name the best hunting cartridge is sort of like asking, "How high is up?" The answer depends on your perspective. No matter what conclusion I reach, there are going to be folks who disagree with my conclusion. To begin with, you have to specify whether you're talking about the best rifle caliber, best handgun cartridge or best shotgun shell. For today, let's just consider what might be the best rifle cartridge. We'll worry about handgun calibers, and shotgun gauges another day.

Since the beginning of modern rifle cartridges in the late 19th century, there have been numerous cartridges that have been used and loved by riflemen around the world. All have pros and cons. It has been claimed that the venerable 30–30 Winchester has taken more deer than any caliber in the world. I suspect that's probably true, and if you're a whitetail hunter in the woods of the eastern U.S., then you'd probably swear that the 30–30 is the world's best cartridge.

However, if you're a fan of hunting Rocky Mountain Elk you'd probably laugh at the puny 30–30 and be much more inclined to favor a 7mm Magnum or a 308 Winchester. Hunters seeking mule deer on the open reaches of the Great Basin may turn to the 270 Winchester as their choice for the best rifle while antelope hunters in the same range may depend upon a 243. Professional guides in Alaska swear by a lever action in 45–70 that will deliver massive stopping power on a charging grizzly at 20 yards.

In short, your definition of the best cartridge will be influenced by the kind of game you hunt, as well as the terrain you hunt in. Varmint hunters prefer a cartridge that shoots a fairly light bullet at amazingly fast speeds. They'll choose cartridges like a 223 Remington or a 25–06, a 22 Hornet or something more esoteric like a 257 Roberts. Varmint hunters need a cartridge that can carry a long distance in a very short time, and thus the slower, heavy bullets needed for bear, elk or moose are almost useless to them. By contrast, a varmint caliber would just make a bear or wild boar angry and could get you killed.

If I had to pick just one caliber to hunt the broadest array of North American game, I have no doubt that I'd choose the 30–06. As its name suggests, it's been around for over 100 years, and it's available everywhere. You can find 30–06 ammo from fancy gun shops to small town hardware stores all over America. You can get light bullets in 06 for varmints and antelope, medium bullets for deer and black bear, and heavy duty bullets for wild boar, grizzlies, and elk. The 30–06 is, in my opinion, the best rifle cartridge in the North America. If you disagree, contact me and tell me why. It might be an interesting discussion.

⌘ ⌘ ⌘

FIRE BUILDING 101

November 2009

One of my favorite short stories is Jack London's "To Build a Fire." The central character of London's short story is a novice woodsman in the Klondike Gold Rush of a hundred years ago. The man falls through the ice of a frozen creek and has only minutes to build a fire and get warm or he will freeze to death. It's a riveting story that still captivates readers. Because of its influence, I have always been fanatical about carrying matches and other fire building materials whenever I venture into the wilderness.

One of my prized possessions is a Marbles Match Safe made by Marbles Arms and Manufacturing of Gladstone, Michigan. Marbles was originally incorporated by Webster Marble in 1898 and is still in business today. Their match safe was patented in 1900 and manufactured until 1970. Original Marbles Match Safes are sought by collectors of early Americana and sell today for under $50.00. Far beyond their value as antiques, they are still a great way to keep your matches dry and be able to build a fire under wet, cold conditions. My match safe is always filled with old fashioned strike anywhere matches.

Reading London's "To Build a Fire" must have made me paranoid because I don't just carry matches to build a fire. I also carry disposable butane lighter, a magnifying glass and a zip-lock bag filled with fire starting tinder (lint from your clothes dryer makes great tinder). Although it doesn't happen very often, there are times when I've gotten soaked by falling in a creek or by being out in a day-long rain. When you're soaking wet and so cold your hands are shaking, being able to build a fire is a huge deal. Heck, it might even be a life and death situation. Whatever the case, I'm not taking any chances.

As youngsters, my buddies and I would be out in the woods at every opportunity. Early one spring we were able to convince our parents to drop us off at the top of Ebbets Pass for an over night camping adventure in 6 feet of snow. We built a fire, cooked our dinner, and told the usual campfire stories until it was time to turn in for the night.

Naturally, being raised on the Smokey Bear model, we made sure our fire was dead out. Trust me, never pee on a fire when you're downwind! The temperature that night was about 20 degrees below zero, and soon all of us were freezing cold in our summer sleeping bags. Finally, we got up to relight the fire and avoid hypothermia, only the wet wood wouldn't burn. We tried everything, but no fire.

Finally, I had the bright idea that we could slit open shotgun shells and get some loose gunpowder to help start the fire. Gunpowder only explodes when it's confined in a tight space. Sprinkled loosely over tinder and topped with kindling, loose gunpowder just burns with a bright flame and starts a fire very handily.

Knowing the used shotgun shells were empty, we proceeded to toss them into the fire. Imagine our surprise when they began to merrily explode just like firecrackers! We forgot about the unfired primers in the shot shells and were enjoying the free fireworks display until one of the exploding primers shot me right below the knee! It sailed right through my pant leg material and burned a nice neat little circle pattern in my leg which I still have to this day. If you ever see me wearing shorts, I'll be glad to show you my primer scar. Throwing empty shot shells is near the top of my list of really stupid things never to do again.

They say that the painful lessons are the ones you remember longest. In any event, the next time you go afield, be sure to take adequate fire starting materials with you. It ensures that you won't run the risk of hypothermia in the snow or freezing rain. Just don't blow yourself up in the process!

⌘ ⌘ ⌘

HANDGUN BASICS

December 2009

A couple weeks ago I discussed what I thought was the best rifle cartridge ever invented. Today let's consider the pros and cons of handguns. In my earlier years I was a fishing fanatic, and fished at every opportunity. Among the mountain of gear I always carried with me was a 22 revolver. The first chamber of my 22 was loaded with birdshot in case I suddenly happened upon a coiled rattler. I would draw and fire as a reflex action, without even a conscious thought. At a range of 10 feet, you don't even need to aim, you instinctively hit the snake every time. Birdshot at close range will vaporize a deadly rattler instantly. That little 22 probably sent a dozen rattlers to meet their maker.

Of course, not everybody is crazy enough to tramp along lonely streams in search of trout almost every waking hour. As years passed I began to hunt more and eventually ended up chasing bears through the woods. My brother-in- law was a professional bear guide and had introduced me to bear hunting with hounds. There are no fat bear hunters, nor are there any sane bear hunters. These guys are truly crazy and care more about their hounds than they do about their own lives. I have seen numerous houndsmen wade into the middle of a fight between bear and dogs and reach in to grab their dogs off an enraged bear.

Many serious bear hunters carry a handgun rather than a rifle. A handgun is lighter to carry and easier to use at close range. Shooting a bear is simple–you stick your handgun in the bear's ear and pull the trigger. No kidding! That's really how it's done. Up close and personal. In tight quarters like that, a rifle just gets in the way.

What kind of handgun do you use for bears? Almost any revolver from 38 special on up to the big 500 caliber monsters will work for bears. Personally, I prefer a 357 magnum built by Dan Wesson. It's my belief that in hunting, a revolver is superior to the automatic. If you have a dud or a misfire, you simply pull the trigger once more, and a new cartridge rotates into place. An automatic can get you killed when you're 2 feet from an angry bear or a 300 pound hog comes charging out of the brush. The old revolver works every time and will never let you down.

Fortunately, I have never had to fire a gun at another human being, and I hope I never do. Unfortunately, there are anti-social people out there who can and do harm their fellow humans on a regular basis. Some occupations are dangerous and so are some neighborhoods, and there can be times when you need a handgun for self defense. If that's the case, and you feel you must carry a gun with you, that's where the automatic pistol earns its keep. They are convenient to carry and, with proper training and lots of practice, a most effective self defense weapon.

What caliber to use? Whatever caliber you feel most comfortable with. For example, I am a large guy with big hands and feel perfectly at home shooting a 45 auto. A woman with a slight build might feel more comfortable using a 380 auto that has less recoil and fits her hand better. There's even a reasonably good argument that a 22 automatic purse gun is well suited for personal defense.

Whatever caliber you choose and whichever style gun you shoot, the most important factor is practice, practice, practice. Join a shooting club like the Manteca Sportsmen. They even have free classes for beginners and are very reasonable to join. Most towns have a range of some sort, check under "gun ranges" in Google and then type in your town. You'll find one. Handguns can be fun, convenient, and maybe even a lifesaver. Check it out.

⌘ ⌘ ⌘

HOME DEFENSE

November 2009

Over the years, I have received much comment from readers about my columns, some of it complimentary, some of it critical. Never, have I received as much feedback as on my recent article "The Obama Factor" in which I observed that ammunition supplies are in extremely short supply everywhere. I have had folks reporting empty ammo shelves in Virginia, Pennsylvania, Nevada, and Arizona just for starters. I believe that, in large part, the nationwide shortage of ammo is because ordinary people are truly scared for the safety of their families. People are afraid that not only can't the government protect us, but also that they're hindering us from protecting ourselves. I was talking to a city councilman the other day who has never owned a gun but who has now decided to get one for home defense.

With the recession in full force, and governments everywhere cutting budgets, it looks like public safety may be up to the individual because the government can't or won't do it. Here in California, Governor Schwarzenegger is talking about laying off prison guards and releasing 35,000 felons into society to save money. He is also considering "borrowing" billions from cities and counties to balance the state budget, leaving local governments to cut public safety as well. The situation is similar across the nation. Folks, we're gonna have to protect ourselves!

For years, one of my in-laws had been an advocate of gun control and genuinely believed that guns should be outlawed. About 5:00 one morning Jim was out in his driveway preparing to leave for an early flight, when he came face to face with two characters who had just finished burglarizing the neighbor's house. A few hours later, he was on the phone asking me what kind of gun I'd suggest for home defense. I resisted the temptation to say "I told you so,' and concentrated instead on giving him the best answer I could.

A number of weapon choices came to mind, and I was having difficulty trying to decide what would be the best gun to recommend. Finally, it dawned on me that the best weapon for self defense logically varies, depending upon the background and needs of the user. Basically, your choice of weapon should probably relate to your overall familiarity with guns. If you are a military veteran you might feel comfortable with a forty five automatic pistol, whereas if you are a regular duck or pheasant hunter, you'd probably feel right at home with your scatter-gun. If, however, you've never owned a gun before and are terrified of guns, you might well be best off just getting a good burglar alarm.

Assuming that you've had limited experience with guns, but feel you want to get one for **home** defense, I believe that there is one clear choice for a novice. For household defense, there is nothing, and I **do** mean nothing, more effective than a pump action shotgun. While a double barreled shotgun is probable easier to operate, there are a number of pump shotguns being made today especially for self defense. No one in his right mind ever wants to have to fire a gun at another human being, but if your life or family is threatened, there is no more effective weapon at close range than a shotgun. Perhaps the best feature of all is the psychological effect produced by the sound of a shell being jacked into a pump shotgun. Just the sound alone could save your life because it's an unmistakable sound that will raise the hair on the back of your neck and make you want to get far away as quickly as possible.

OK, shotguns are great for home defense, but what if you work or have to travel through an unsafe area, and want to carry a gun for defense? My brother once worked at night in the rail-yards of a large inner city and was regularly in danger of assault. In a situation like that a handgun is clearly the most logical choice simply because it's easier to carry. A gun will not save your life if you haven't got it with you.

Once again, however, your temperament and background come into play. Some folks are comfortable with a big caliber handgun like a 45 or a 357 magnum while others would be best off with a small 22 automatic that can fit easily into a purse or pocket. It's my opinion that the 25 caliber automatic is probably the most useless cartridge in the world. I would never recommend that anyone get a 25 auto for any reason. If you really need a fishing weight that badly, get a proper lead weight at a fishing shop. Bear in mind that if you're going to carry a **concealed** gun, you must get a concealed weapon permit from your police chief or sheriff. Contact your local police chief if you live in the city limits or your sheriff if you live in the unincorporated county.

If you acquire **any** gun for home or personal defense it is imperative that you take the time to become familiar with it. Get on the range and thoroughly acquaint yourself with your weapon. Fire several boxes of shells through your gun and practice, practice, practice. Practice until you are completely comfortable with it. For assistance consult a qualified firearms instructor. Here in Ripon, we're fortunate to have a first class indoor range and gunshop with dedicated professionals at The Barnwood Arms on Main Street. In other areas contact either your local gunshop or the N.R.A. at 1-800-672-3888. Once you've selected a weapon that's right for you and become comfortable using it, you can sleep a little more soundly at night knowing that if the need arose, you'd be prepared to defend the lives of you and your loved ones.

⌘ ⌘ ⌘

RELOADING

January 2010

On New Year's Day, my son, Bo, and I went out to do a little target shooting. I always like to get a new year off to a good start by doing something in the outdoors. It really doesn't matter whether its trout fishing in Yosemite where there's year-round trout season, striper fishing in the Delta or boar hunting in the coastal hills, as long as I'm out in the fresh air doing something active I'm happy as can be.

After we had finished our practice shooting session, we had completely depleted my supply of 7 millimeter ammunition. Bo suggested that we reload a new batch of ammo so that we'd have plenty for the next time we wanted to go shooting. Before long we had a table erected in the family room and had it covered with boxes of empty brass cartridges, reloading tools, powder and primers. For the next hour or so, we had a great time.

We talked about the ballistics of the 7 x 57 mm cartridge and how it was one of the first modern loads invented. The 7 x 57 Mauser was such a good load in such a superior gun that it vastly outperformed all of the military cartridges of the day. That's not just my opinion; it was also the opinion of Teddy Roosevelt and his Rough Riders who faced the 7mm Mauser in Cuba. As president, one of the first things Roosevelt did was order the Army to develop a cartridge that could out perform that darned Mauser cartridge. As a result, the 30–06 Springfield was born. The U.S. government actually paid a royalty to the Mauser Company because the hot new cartridge used a Mauser action in order to handle the higher pressures. Even today almost all modern bolt action rifles are based upon the incredibly strong 1898 Mauser action.

As Bo and I were loading cartridges we also were very careful to examine each brass case to make sure it hadn't developed any hairline cracks or suspicious looking bulges in the brass. Reloading is deadly serious, and you can't afford to make any mistakes. We check and double check every round for safety.

Sure enough, we found a round that we had loaded with a new primer and a new bullet but we had somehow managed to overlook putting in the gunpowder. Had we not caught it, such a load (called a squib) would have had just enough energy from the detonation of the primer, to shoot a bullet about halfway up the barrel. Then, if you failed to detect the situation, on your next shot your rifle barrel might just explode a few inches in front of your face. I remember a fellow in Tracy who made a similar mistake and lost a couple fingers and one eye. That's why I teach my son that you can never be too safe.

In our reloading session we made several different kinds of loads. We loaded a 160 grain cartridge that is just about ideal for mule deer. Then we loaded a 140 grain batch that is super for both antelope and blacktail deer, some 180 grain loads for boar hunting, and finally, a batch of little 100 grain hollow points that are devastating on varmints.

A couple of my farming friends really don't like to use poison bait to control the squirrels on their ranches. But if they let the squirrel population get out of hand, the little critters can destroy a nut crop. It's hard to believe the damage an unchecked squirrel population can wreak on a nut orchard. By using our 100 grain hollow point loads we can get lots of rifle practice, keep the squirrels from destroying a crop, and not pollute the environment with poison.

Reloading your own ammunition not only gives you precision loads for specific uses, but it also saves you a lot of money. I figure that by reloading my own ammunition my cost per shot is probably 25% of the cost of store bought ammo. Don't get to feeling too sorry for Joe Mangelos at the Barnwood Gun Shop. Since I buy all my powder, primers, and reloading equipment from Joe, I figure he's pretty happy too. If you wanted to get started reloading your own ammunition, Joe will be glad to make an appointment with the factory representative who supplies the reloading equipment. It's not really too costly to get started and once you get up and running you'll soon save quite a bit.

For me, reloading provides a chance for my son and me to talk for hours. We discuss math and science in the form of ballistics, and history and safety and all of the other sorts of things that fathers ands sons should be talking about. If you want an opportunity to save money, get cartridges loaded exactly to fit your needs, and spend time with your kids, take up reloading. You won't be sorry.

⌘ ⌘ ⌘

Section Six
HUNTING

BOW HUNTING

July 1982

As I was walking back from my favorite brook trout stream, last Sunday, I saw something unusual out of the corner of my eye and went to investigate. About 15 feet up in a large pine tree was a wooden platform. The entire platform was carpeted and looked pretty comfortable. It was made of 2x4's and extended out on two sides of the tree. Someone had gone to a lot of trouble to pack that lumber over a mile from the road through pretty rough country. Why do you suppose someone would do that? Bowhunting, that's why.

Bowhunting for deer in the Sierra Nevada will open on August 21. More and more hunters are taking up bow hunting. With modern rifles, one has the capability to shoot a deer out to several hundred yards. Why, then, would you handicap yourself by using an ancient form of weapon which automatically stacks the cards in the deer's favor? Knowledgeable bow hunters, when asked that question, will smile and say, "That's exactly the reason! Because it is so much more difficult, the challenge is ten times greater."

In order to get within bow range of a deer, you have to become a better hunter in almost every respect. You must know the habits of your quarry better so that you can put yourself in the right place at the right time. You must learn to stalk better and move through the woods without alarming either the deer or the birds and squirrels who so readily give the alarm. You must learn to reduce the effect of human scent and always watch for wind currents that can betray you. You must also master the art of camouflage so that you become invisible in the surrounding scenery.

Nearly any normal person can learn to shoot a rifle with reasonable accuracy in a fairly short time but not with a bow, whereas proficiency with a bow takes years of practice. When I first began bow hunting, I practiced for almost a year before I considered myself good enough to go hunting. Even with all my practice, I still restricted my shots to no further than forty yards.

Many times I have stalked to within 50 or 60 yards of legal bucks, and had I been carrying a rifle, it would have been a simple matter to shoot one. The challenges of bow hunting are so great, that even being able to get within shooting range is a triumph in itself! About 15 years ago, I stalked to within 35 yards of a buck. I was sure that the pounding of my heart would scare him away. I drew back the bow, anchored the arrow, and thought to myself, "This is it" and released my arrow. "Thunk" went the arrow as it sunk into a tree a few inches over the buck's back. The deer was gone before I could get a second shot. The deer had won, but in a way, so had I, just by getting close enough for a shot.

Somehow, I haven't been able to find sufficient time to practice with my bow for the past dozen years and thus have not been bowhunting lately. Every once in awhile, I look up at the dust-covered bow on my wall or run my finger over my camouflage clothing in the back closet. I keep telling myself, "Maybe I'll start practicing again so I can go bow hunting next fall." I have too much respect for the deer to hunt for them if I'm not adequately prepared. Even though I no longer bowhunt myself, I have the greatest respect for those who have the dedication, perseverance and skill to call themselves bowhunters. I salute you!

⌘ ⌘ ⌘

PHEASANT HUNTING

November 1985

"Cold, Good God, it's cold." I said to myself as I looked out across the fog. There's something about fog that seems to creep in around your sleeves and cuffs and collars. I don't know if it's real or just psychological, but fog chills me clear to the bone.

This is it, the day I've been awaiting for weeks now, the opening of pheasant season. I was hoping for the morning to dawn clear and crisp and sunny cold, but the fog is everywhere. We start in a picked over pepper field west of Linden. We begin to walk abreast, six rows apart. The mud sticks to the bottom of our boots and builds up higher and higher until it feels as though we're walking on stilts. It doesn't do any good to kick it off because it just builds back up again.

The moisture from the wet plants soaks you from the knee down. As you walk, you feel the "crunch" of the fallen peppers underfoot, making a distinct "pop" when stepped on. Quiet banter flows up and down the line between the hunters. "Hey, Bob," someone says, "Remember the time a pheasant flushed right in front of you and you pointed your gun and hollered, "Bang, bang and forgot to pull the trigger? Hoo boy, that was great!"

"Oh, yeah," comes the reply, "I remember the dove hunt when you earned the nickname 'Meadowlark.'" The talk subsides as we approach the end of the field. If they're in here, this is when they'll flush. Any minute now, easy, gun ready. Each crunch of a pepper underfoot now sounds as loud as a firecracker. Nothing! Not one bird! Dang!

We move on into a walnut orchard. Suddenly, a large shape comes flying out of the fog. "Hold it!" somebody yells, "it's only a barn owl." The owl lumbers off slowly and disappears into the mist. We begin to make a second pass back through the pepper field and flush a rabbit but still no pheasants. One guy hollers to our host, "Hey Meatball, you make any money on these peppers?" The owner replies, "Hell, no, I just plant em so you clowns will have a place to hunt."

As we approach the end of the peppers, a hush again falls over the hunters. A pheasant flushes at the far end. Boom! Boom! Boom! Two more birds flush off the right end, and the two guys next to me empty their guns. Three hunters have fired nine shots, and all three birds sail off unruffled into the fog. Oh well, we got plenty of exercise and some great companionship It was a good morning anyway.

Just as we were about to pack it in for the day, Francis suggested that he and I take one last try in a couple of acres of weeds. The weeds are pretty thick, so we move closer together because the birds are more likely to just hunker down and sit tight instead of fly. We reach the end of the weed patch and make a last turn back toward the trucks. There he is! Twenty yards out and heading away to the left! Easy now, swing the gun from behind, pass the bird, keep swinging, Fire! Got him! Off to the right come three or four more shots and Francis has his bird too. I can't believe it—I actually got my bird on the first shot.

All right, pheasant for dinner tonight! With a little rice and some gravy, a gourmet delight. Of course, I'll save the feathers for tying trout flies and making hat bands. Nothing's going to waste from this bird. Later that evening, when swirling a snifter of brandy around in front of the fire, I feel comfortably full and content, Yes, indeed, pheasant hunting is all right.

⌘ ⌘ ⌘

THE BOAR FACTS

November 1998

Over the last few years I have seen increasing numbers of wild pigs while out on my outdoor excursions. As I understand it, wild pigs weren't very common in California until William Randolph Hearst imported some Russian wild boar to stock his private game preserve at Hearst Castle. Apparently everything went along fine and dandy until the boar refused to cooperate and escaped into the surrounding countryside. Over the years the Russian Boar began to breed with escaped barnyard pigs that had escaped from neighboring farms.

For a couple decades it seemed as though nothing was happening, but the hybrid pigs, known as feral pigs to Fish and Game biologists, were merrily breeding away and expanding their numbers in the wild back country of the coastal mountains. Pretty soon the pigs were making a nuisance of themselves by tearing up crops and fences in semi-civilized properties. It was about the late 50s that pig hunting began to become popular both on the central coast, and Catalina Island.

Hunting guide services soon became available and word began to get out that wild pigs were pretty darned good game animals. They are smart, fast, incredibly edible, and make a great looking wall mount. To top it all off, the pig population is growing by leaps and bounds. By the late 70s the pigs had spread across the coastal valleys and into the fringes of the great central valley.

Until about a dozen years ago I had only hunted wild pigs at Fort Hunter Liggett over on the coast. Although I hunted my little heart out, the only glimpse I got of a wild pig was at the check-out station at Hunter Liggitt where the successful hunters weighed out their animals. Boy, was I impressed! Those wild boars were the biggest, nastiest, ugliest critters I had ever seen. Still, however, those darned pigs turned out to be smarter than me, and I got nowhere for several years.

During the last few years, however, wild pigs have become increasingly numerous on the ranches where I catch rattlers. I began to carry a 357 magnum handgun, just in case I might run across a boar at close range. I finally began to get shots at the wild pigs but, once again, the pigs have proven smarter or faster than me, and I've missed several shots at running boar 75 to 100 yards away. OK, so I'm not a great pistol shot. Still, hitting a moving target at over 50 yards is a pretty hard trick with a handgun.

Getting afflicted worse and worse with boar fever, I began to carry my old 7 millimeter Mauser carbine with me. About two months ago I missed a running shot at a huge boar about 400 yards away. I didn't feel too bad about missing because that's a long shot even for a good rifleman. Then, a month ago, I missed a couple uphill shots at forty yards that any idiot should have made. It's really embarrassing when your son says, "Gee, Dad, next time you should take a little more time and aim more carefully." This pig hunting can sure be humiliating.

Finally, on Memorial Day weekend, I spotted a nice pig standing broadside at about 50 yards away. This time I did everything right and actually shot my very first wild pig. This time, my son's comment was, "All right Dad, great shot!" What a thrill! Although the sow I got was only average and weighed about 150 pounds on the hoof, I'm still almost as excited as a new bridegroom.

I could get into this wild pig stuff. It's pretty darned exciting. Now I've got to get a really BIG one. I heard that one of the guys on a neighboring ranch shot an old boar that went over 800 pounds. Now there's a goal!

⌘ ⌘ ⌘

THE BLONDE BEAR

September 2007

Here's a memory test for you. Do you remember reading *Moby Dick* in High School? Or maybe you recall the movie *Moby Dick* with Gregory Peck that came out about 1956? If you can remember that far back, you'll recall that Captain Ahab was obsessed with finding and killing his nemesis, the great white whale.

While I hope I'm not quite as fanatical as Captain Ahab, I too have a nemesis that haunts me, the "blonde bear." I don't know if you were aware of it or not, but our American black bears aren't always black. *Ursus Americanus*, which is native to almost all of our 50 states, comes in a variety of color phases from coal black to snow white, and every variation in between. Probably the rarest color is white, and there is a sub-variety of black bear that frequents the glaciers of the Northwest Pacific area known as the Blue Glacier Bear. The emblem of California the California grizzly is sometimes referred to as the California golden bear.

Several years ago while deer hunting in the Sierra Nevada; I spotted a very large blonde bear. When hunting I almost always use a rifle sling and I was too slow getting my rifle off my shoulder. By the time I was ready to shoot, the blonde bear had vanished behind a large boulder. Closer investigation revealed a perfect den site where several large boulders had fallen together to form a protected cavity just the right size to shelter a bear for the winter.

Although I hunted that mountainside heavily that fall, I never again caught sight of the blonde bear. In the wild, the average black bear lives about 3 or 4 years, although under the right conditions they can reach the ripe old age of 10 or 12. Genetics being what they are, even if my blonde bear has gone on to that big berry patch in the sky, I still hold out hope that his offspring are out there prowling his old mountain. Several years have now passed and I still haven't gotten him, but every fall I'll be back on the mountain looking for him.

Albinos in nature are not really that unusual. I have seen albino foxes, deer, and even snakes. Legend has it that the Plains Indians revered the White Buffalo as having mystical powers. The opposite of an albino is an even rarer anomaly due to melanism, which causes animals to be jet black. Although I have never knowingly seen one in the wild, I have seen a melanistic all black mule deer in a museum in Nevada. Whatever his attributes, the blonde bear has drawn me back to his territory time after time. Like Captain Ahab, I'm going to get that blonde bear if it kills me.

⌘ ⌘ ⌘

HUNTING WITH HOUNDS

June 2008

The older I get, the faster time seems to fly. It seems like only yesterday that I was chasing my first bear in the woods near Hoopa, California. It's hard to believe that it's now been just over 30 years ago. Last fall my son Donald and I were once again out in the woods running after bears. Without a doubt the best way to catch a bear is to use trained hounds. While it may sound like it's a simple matter to just shoot a bear once the hounds have treed him, nothing could be farther from the truth. Hunting with hounds is a time consuming, complicated, yet uniquely American tradition.

When you begin your bear hunt you cruise endless miles of backwoods roads in a pickup that's heavily modified just for bear hunting. The easiest clue to recognizing a bear hunter's truck is the dog box in the truck bed. It usually holds about 6 bear hounds and has a platform on top of it so that 2 to 4 dogs can ride on top of the box. Fanatical bear hunters glue indoor/outdoor carpet to the hood of their truck and then affix an eyebolt on each side. Then two more dogs are leashed to the hood of the truck as well. As you drive along at about 2 miles per hour, the dogs sniff the air constantly for bear scent. The noses on bear hounds are nothing short of amazing. Imagine yourself walking across town to the local shopping center. Now imagine that 2 or 3 days later a good dog can smell your scent and trace your exact route. That's kind of how it works with bears.

The key is to search and search until you find a fresh scent that's only a few hours old. The dogs get all excited and begin to bark in anticipation. You get out and examine the ground for fresh tracks, or even better yet for steaming bear droppings. Upon finding a fresh track the dogs are released and the work begins. If the bear goes down the canyon, so do the dogs and so do you. If the bear runs over the next ridge, so do you. You run and run until you think you're gonna drop, and then you run some more. I have observed very few fat bear hunters.

Sometimes you get lucky and tree a bear within a few hundred yards. More often than not they run until you're exhausted, and then they "tree." As you approach the treed bear after running 5 miles, your heart is pounding and your gun is bouncing up and down with your heartbeat. You take a close look at the bear and find that he is too small for that rug you wanted or that his coat is all mangy or the wrong color. So you gather up the dogs and trek back to the truck to start over. Eventually, you find a bear that looks just right.

Sometimes the bear doesn't cooperate and comes down the tree into the middle of frantically barking dogs. That's when you discover how crazy bear hunters really are. They care more about their dogs than they do about their own safety. The houndsman will jump without hesitation into the middle of a bear and dogs fight to save their dogs. They wade right in and begin pulling dogs off a highly agitated bear. You can always tell if you're talking to a real houndsman when he begins to roll up his sleeve (or pants leg) to show you his scars. Another indicator is when he takes out his glass eye, or shows you the teeth marks on his gunstock. That's a real bear hunter.

A piece of really good advice is never to shoot a large bear unless he's **uphill** from the truck. Anyway you slice it, dragging a big bear uphill is hard work. It is vital to get your bear cleaned and skinned immediately so that the meat doesn't spoil. Get that bear to the butcher as soon as possible, and you will enjoy some great eating all year long. Jake Berghorst at Austin Meat Service does a fantastic job with bear sausage as well as the steaks, roasts and chops. I have bear sausage at least once a week and bear steaks almost all year long. Just about the time the meat starts running low it's time for bear season again.

If you don't know a houndsman to assist you or you want to learn more about how to get started in hunting California bears, you should plan to attend the big houndsman's dinner this year at the Ripon Community Center on July 29. Tickets are only $40.00 a person and all the money goes into conservation of bears and their habitat. There are great auction items and raffle prizes and the food and camaraderie are great. I'll be there and bidding on one of the great guided bear trips. For ticket information see the gang at the Barnwood Arms in Ripon. Hunting with hounds is extremely exciting, and the Ripon Houndsman's Dinner is a great way to get hooked on this uniquely American tradition. SEE YOU THERE!

⌘ ⌘ ⌘

HARVEST TIME

September 2009

I ran into an almond grower the other day and inquired if he had begun his harvest. "Yup," he replied, "Just started shaking the first trees about an hour ago." Harvest season is definitely upon us. I know that a lot of folks hate to see summer go, but I love the coming of all of the seasons. I love the cool mornings that are the first hint of fall, the first frost that warns of the coming of winter, and the warm afternoon sun that signals the advent of spring.

Way back when almost everyone was a farmer, the fall harvest and the fall hunting season went hand in hand. As a people, we were all aware, on a day-to-day, year-to-year, basis that we were part of God's grand scheme. Just as droughts, spring floods, or an especially bitter winter created lean times for farmers, so, too, the whims of nature meant lean hunting or a bumper crop of game for the winter.

Times, of course, have changed, and we are now predominantly an urban society instead of an agricultural one. Rather than living and working on farms, most of us now live in cities and work at jobs that leave us out of contact with the workings of nature and her eternal cycles.

One touchstone to the natural world that many urban dwellers retain is our hunting heritage. Every fall millions of Americans take to the woods and fields and experience being a part of nature, rather than being insulated from nature. Indeed, many Americans who are neither farmers nor hunters seem to feel they are above nature rather than part of it.

It's those urban dwellers who are so insulated from nature that give us a society that thinks dairy farming or chicken farms are a form of animal cruelty. They don't seem to realize that if you order bacon and eggs at Denny's and wash it down with a glass of milk that farming somehow must have entered the picture. The fact is, those are the same folks who condemn hunting too. Farmers and hunters not only have a lot of similarities and are often the same people.

To succeed as a hunter, you must know something about the game you seek and the environment that surrounds it. You must study the terrain, the vegetation your quarry needs for food and shelter, and age old migration routes. You must be aware of the importance of a shift in the wind or a subtle rustle in the leaves, while in an urban environment you can pay no attention to the weather and only suffer inconvenience or perhaps a cold. When afield, however, ignoring natures warning signs can prove fatal. If you get too wrapped up in tracking a deer and fail to notice the wind shifting from west to south, you might just get trapped in the first blizzard of the season.

Every farmer knows that he is subject to the changing moods of nature, that a freak storm or frost or rain can spell disaster. A farmer who ignores the signs of a coming frost is likely to pay a heck of a price. City dwellers have become insulated from the natural world. The seeming security of our comfortable homes, air conditioned cars and processed TV dinners have lulled us into forgetting that we are still a part of that esoteric term "the balance of nature." We know that water springs clean and clear from our kitchen tap, that milk comes from the supermarket, and that meat comes wrapped in plastic wrap.

I honestly believe that a large number of us have forgotten that water must come from a well or a river, that milk is the product of a living, breathing, animal and that if we eat meat for dinner then some animal had to die. It seems to me that those millions of Americans who go afield each fall probably have a better understanding of the value of clean streams or the importance of a meadow where deer can have their fawns. Whether seeking deer with a bow, or pheasants with a shotgun, hunters realize that we must kill if we are to eat meat.

Each fall, those of us who hunt have re-educated ourselves and once again learned that we are indeed a part of this planet on which we live. Buying our meat at the supermarket is all well and good, but hunters and anglers, at least in part, stay connected to the cycles of nature. When we succeed, and sit down to a dinner of venison or trout, which we have been fortunate enough to put on the table, maybe, just maybe, we might be a little more likely to give thanks for our meal.

⌘ ⌘ ⌘

Section Seven
POTPOURRI

FAREWELL TO A FRIEND

September 1982

Because of the early exposure my parents gave me to the outdoors, it was probably inevitable that I would grow to love wild places. I also learned to love reading at an early age by perusing almost every comic book in my Dad's drug store on a regular basis. It is not surprising, therefore, that my love for both the outdoors and reading would merge into my being hopelessly hooked on outdoor magazines by the time I was 12 or 13 years old.

It seemed as though I really got to know some of the people who wrote the outdoor articles. They shared their experiences with me, their likes and dislikes and even their morals. I learned about fishing from men like Ray Bergman and about hunting from Jack O'Connor and Clyde Ormond and Warren Paige. My favorite writer of all was Ted Trueblood, who wrote for *Field and Stream.*

I don't know if it was a matter of cause and effect, but I liked Trueblood because he thought like I did. He loved small streams where a 12 inch trout was a trophy to be proud of. He loved wild and lonely places where his companions were God's creations. I remember once Ted wrote about how he delighted in sending cards to friends postmarked from Happy Camp, a small community in Northern California.

I so enjoyed the writings of these extraordinary people who were willing to share their outdoor lives with me, that eventually it entered my mind that I should do the same. I read every book I could find on how to write, and especially on how to write about the outdoors. I put ideas to paper and finally wrote what's known as a query letter, outlining to an editor the idea I had for an article.

I sent my first query letter to Ted Trueblood. Weeks dragged by, and finally a reply arrived. Ted began by saying that he was only a columnist and field editor (whatever that was), and that my letter had been rerouted from New York to his home in Nampa, Idaho. He went on to explain that he had forwarded my query to Editor Jack Samson in New York. Ted then proceeded to praise my query letter and encourage me to hang in there and not be discouraged despite the rejection slips that every writer gets too many of.

Anyone who's ever tried his hand at writing has undoubtedly gotten his share of rejection slips. Sure enough, my first article was rejected, but after all, Ted Trueblood had encouraged me, and besides at least the editor thought enough of my query to have me write the article. So I persevered, and eventually I got my first magazine article accepted and published. I sent a copy of that first article to Ted and thanked him for encouraging me. Even though we had last corresponded years earlier, Ted remembered me and was gracious enough to compliment me and encourage me once again.

Recently I picked up my copy of *Field and Stream* and immediately turned to Trueblood's column. I couldn't believe it—Ted Trueblood was dead. I thought of all the times we had had shared together; of the trout fishing, and the bird hunting, and the campfires. Now, suddenly, it would be no more.

I suppose it's ironic that we never actually met face-to-face, but that's probably the mark of a great writer, he makes you feel as though you really know him. I know that I'm not alone, that there are thousands of folks out there who feel that they, too, knew Ted Trueblood. They've camped, and fished, and hunted with him just as I have, and they know that the world was a better place because Ted Trueblood shared his corner of it with us. So long Ted, we're gonna miss you.

⌘ ⌘ ⌘

GUN CONTROL

October 1982

Once, when I was out fishing, I accidentally stepped on a hornet's nest. It was really scary while the air around me was filled with angry hornets. I was able to dive into a river and only received 6 or 8 stings. You'd think after an experience like that I'd have the sense not to intentionally stir up a hornet's nest. Well, that's what I'm going to do right now.

Coming up in the November election is a gun control initiative for the people to vote on. Gun control is an emotional issue and as such it is difficult to deal with on a rational basis. It would not surprise me in the slightest to receive numbers of angry letters and phone calls, many of them anonymous. Nonetheless, it is an issue of considerable importance and should be discussed. I may as well state right now that I am opposed to this particular initiative (Proposition 15) because it is extremely poorly written, and that I am opposed to gun control in general because it just doesn't work.

It appears to me that there are two basic issues relative to gun control: first, reduction of violent crime, and second, the infringement of individual liberties. The reason given for most gun control attempts is that it will reduce crime. On the surface, that sounds logical enough—less guns, less crime. Right? Wrong!

According to the FBI's Uniform Crime Reports, Boston became the nation's most violent city some time after it passed restrictive gun laws. New York City has had a virtual ban on the use of handguns since 1911, and it is the second most violent city in the nation. Proponents of gun control like to point to foreign countries which have restrictive gun laws and low crime rates as proof that gun control works. They very conveniently overlook the fact that countries like Norway, Switzerland, and Israel all have a far higher gun ownership rate and a far lower crime rate than the United States. Due to societal differences, such comparisons are of very little value.

Perhaps you've seen the bumper sticker that says, "When guns are outlawed, only outlaws will have guns." There really is considerable truth in that statement. Do you really think that convicted felons are going to give up their guns which they aren't legally allowed to have now? Firearms actually save lives when used in self defense.

A national survey published in the congressional record in 1979 found that some 13 million Americans live in homes in which a family member has had to use a gun in defense of self, family, or property, from another person. In this and other nearby communities, we are fortunate to have darned fine law enforcement people. But even though we have good cops, they can't be everywhere at once, and we may, at some point in time, have to defend ourselves.

Even if gun control really worked and reduced crime (which it doesn't), it would still be an infringement of your liberties. Those who wish to ignore the Second Amendment guarantees of the right to keep and bear arms by claiming that it only applies to militias should know that to the framers of the Constitution, the militia was synonymous with the people. Thomas Jefferson said, "No free man shall ever be debarred the use of arms." Samuel Adams wanted a constitutional amendment that would guarantee "that the Constitution shall never be constructed to prevent the people of the United States who are peaceable citizens from keeping their own arms."

James Madison said that Americans had the advantage of being armed "unlike other governments which are afraid to trust their people with arms." Perhaps Madison was right. Who knows? Maybe, if 100,000 Poles had guns instead of gun control, Poland would be free today. Some people say it can't happen here, but millions of European Jews thought the same thing.

One of the characters in the best selling novel *Fail Safe* observed that if every Jew had met the Gestapo at the door with a gun there wouldn't have been millions of dead Jews. For those of you who think it can't happen here, remember just a few years ago when the FBI was bugging the phones of private citizens like movie stars, taping the sex lives of civil rights leaders and even burglarizing the offices of people's psychiatrists.

Do you really think it can't happen here? My favorite place in Washington, D.C., is the Jefferson Memorial which is beautifully situated on the banks of the Potomac River. Inscribed on the wall are Jefferson's words—"Eternal vigilance is the price of Liberty."

⌘ ⌘ ⌘

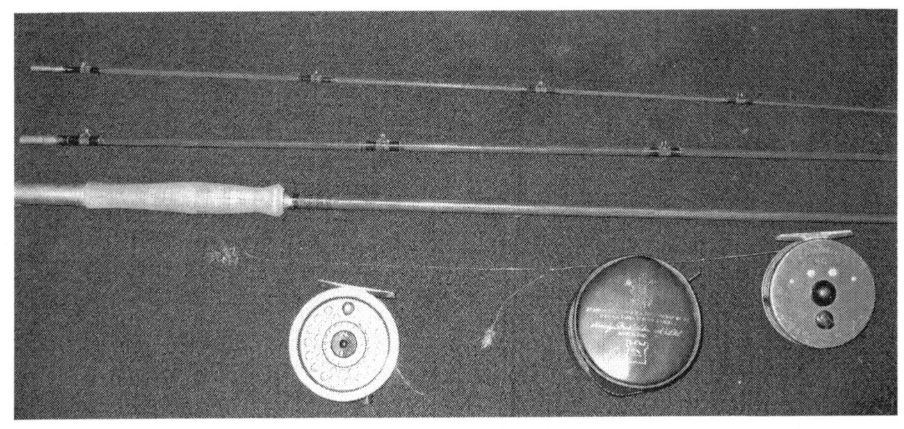

Custom Rod by E.C. Powell
Circa 1920

ANGLING ANTIQUES

August 1984

The other night at the Lion's Club spaghetti dinner, I ran into Wes Stouffer, our conversation turned to fishing and then to fishing antiques. Please don't misunderstand me; I'm not suggesting that Wes is fishing antique. He does, however, fish with an antique split bamboo fly rod that was made just about the time of World War I.

Some time ago I was fortunate enough to obtain an assortment of antique fishing gear that gave me some insight into its previous owner. Examining that gear was like finding a treasure trove of angling history. Digging through the prized possessions of an angler long since passed on, I felt like archeologist Howard Carter digging up King Tut's Tomb. As I handled each individual item, I began to piece together not only a feel for my anonymous angler but also a history of fishing from a time gone by. Each fly, each fly tying tool, each accessory, was like finding another piece of a jigsaw puzzle.

The leaders in the tackle box were a perfect example. They were gut leaders manufactured by Hardy Brothers of Alnwick, England, angling purveyors "by appointment to His Majesty King George V." Gut leaders were fine except that they had to be kept damp or they would get brittle and break. If you were poor you carried your extra leader coiled up in your mouth. But if you were affluent, you had a leader wallet with felt pages you kept wet and carried your gut leaders coiled between the damp pages.

The split bamboo rod of our unknown angler tells a similar story. Contrary to popular belief, not all bamboo rods are valuable. Prior to World War II, almost all rods were made of split bamboo. Some were excellent and costly, some were good medium priced rods, and some were cheap junk. South Bend, Heddon, and Montague were all rods that were comparable to Fords or Chevrolets. They were good serviceable rods manufactured and priced to sell to the multitudes. Lousy rods were usually made in Japan and carried no manufacturer's name at all; while great rods were individually hand made and always carried the name of the man who made them. Rods by Payne, Granger, and Powell were akin to paintings by Rembrandt, Van Gough, and Monet. Our unknown angler fished with a pair of custom rods built by E.C. Powell of Marysville, California.

It was obvious that while our mystery angler had no money worries, neither was he a total snob, for he carried gear that could be bought by any ordinary Joe, as long as it was well made and did the job as well as possible. He had a Marbles Match Safe that kept his matches dry, just like any other outdoorsman of the time. He bought snelled hooks from MOWACO, an acronym for Montgomery Ward and Co. He carried split shot from Winchester, Pflueger's ferrule cement, and used Web's line dressing to make his silk fly line float. He used a Thompson fly vise probably because that was the best vise available at any price.

Our mysterious angler was a very cosmopolitan sort. His rod was western, yet his leaders were English as was his Hardy "Model Perfect" reel. His flies were predominantly Eastern patterns like the Jock Scott and Parmachene Belle, yet his fly boxes also contained Western Steelhead patterns like the Skykomish Sunrise and the Silver Hilton. Just the sound of the names of the flies rolling off your tongue conjures up images of exotic far away streams.

We've all heard the expression, "If only these walls could talk," but I'm sure it applies equally to fishing antiques as well. When I examine the old angler's gear, each piece does indeed talk to me. Together, the old angler's antique gear tells an eloquent story of a man and an era long since gone. I wish I'd known them both. But I guess I haven't missed out totally, I've been lucky enough to know my grandfather, and my father, and Wes Stouffer too.

⌘ ⌘ ⌘

WILDLIFE THERAPY

July 1986

Prior to retiring a few years ago, my friend Howard Shideler spent eons raising turkeys. A couple of weeks ago, Howard told me that on his daily walk he regularly comes across one of the coyotes that resides on his property. He described how, at first, the coyote was very spooky and wouldn't let Howard get anywhere near him, but when Howard showed no sign of threatening him, gradually the wild critter let him approach closer and closer. Before you know it, Howard will have that coyote eating out of his hand.

It was obvious from Howard's enthusiasm that he considered the coyote a welcome guest on his premises. When I observed that his attitude was probably far different from back when he was in the turkey business, he agreed with me completely and indicated that he often went to great trouble to eradicate the coyotes in the past.

The interesting thing I found from our conversation was Howard's observation that even though he lost a bird now and then to the coyotes, they only stole a single bird at a time and ate it not far from where they killed it. I suspect that there's a lot of similarity between old Howard and his coyotes. Just as the coyotes only killed to survive, so Howard only killed coyotes when they threatened his livelihood. When I stop and think about it, Howard's a pretty crafty old coyote himself, so I guess they made pretty well-matched adversaries, even though they've settled into what appears to be an amicable truce.

Most people don't realize it, but I'd be willing to bet that there are occasional coyotes within the boundaries of every city in the Central Valley. Every once in a while, I spot a coyote early in the morning while on the way to the office. Such a sight never fails to brighten my day. I guess I associate the wild critters with wild places, even when they're practically within the city limits.

Whenever I see a coyote, I think not of the freeway I'm driving on, nor of the city I'm about to enter, but rather of warm summer nights around the campfire listening to the yip, yip, yip of the coyotes calling back and forth from one ridge to another. For a moment or two, I forget about the traffic, the smog and the hectic day ahead and think instead of open space, clean air and serenity. Who knows? Maybe coyotes are good therapy for stress, tension, and high blood pressure.

While most folks don't give it a heck of a lot of thought, in almost every urban area there's really an amazing array of what I like to refer to as urban wildlife. I've seen deer inside the city limits of Sacramento, waterfront residents in Stockton often have to protect their trees from marauding beavers and residents on the fringes of most of our cities occasionally get their garbage cans raided by hungry raccoons. Don McGeein regularly had a family of possums residing in an old boxcar on his ranch a couple miles outside of Tracy. He even adopted one and brought it home to live in town with him.

If, like me, you are fascinated by wild critters, you can encourage them to visit. Easiest of all wild creatures to entice into your yard are birds. Hummingbird feeders are very effective and easy to care for. Hang one outside your kitchen window and you'll always have entertainment with your meals. Platform type bird feeders are great fun because they draw so many different kinds of birds. My parents probably go through 20 pounds of birdseed a month. One of their favorite tricks is to nail a marshmallow to the feeding platform. It drives the blue jays crazy when they can't pick it up and fly off with it.

Plain old chicken feed is a great attractor not only for birds, but lots of other critters as well. Since my office is located less than a hundred yards from the river, I buy chicken feed by the 20 pound sack and scatter it all around the grounds. Critters that frequent my place include quail, pheasants, cottontails, jack rabbits and ground squirrels. Of course, every once in a while I get an opportunistic predator who'd like to make a meal of my wild guests. Hawks are pretty common and occasionally I get a gopher snake, which I transplant away from the area. I've even seen a fox a couple times.

Naturally, where you live or work will determine to a large part what kind and how many critters you'll be able to attract. Even if you live smack in the middle of the city, there's still hope. Bird feeders will never fail to attract customers and, should you get other visitors, consider them a sort of wildlife bonus. My grandmother lived in the heart of Oakland and almost always had a squirrel raiding her birdfeeder. What the heck, buy a birdfeeder or two, get a sack of chicken feed and give it a try. Wild critters are fascinating, entertaining, and, if you can believe my friend Howard, much better company than the guys at Rotary.

⌘ ⌘ ⌘

WOODCUTTING AND WINTER FIRES

September 2004

I had my first fire of the season the other day. While it really hasn't gotten cold enough yet, with the first rain even if it was a warm one, I at least had an excuse to light a fire. I love sitting next to a fire with a good book, a mug of hot tea, and music in the background. It's even better if there's a good winter storm howling outside. You can enjoy the storm, yet still be nice and comfy next to your fire.

Ever since I've been old enough to hold a chainsaw, I have been cutting my own wood. It is great exercise, it gets you outdoors, and then, come winter you enjoy the fruits of your labor. I have to confess, for a couple years, I got lazy and just called a local wood seller to deliver cured firewood to my driveway. All that time, however, I was feeling guilty, and finally had to give in and start cutting my own wood again. In addition to the feel-good reasons for doing your own woodcutting, at a price exceeding $200 a cord, there's a serious financial incentive as well.

Bear in mind, that now is not the time to begin your woodcutting season. Now is the time to enjoy your fires. Now is also a good time to begin planning for next season's woodcutting. Growing up in the San Joaquin valley, we used to have an abundance of orchards: cherry, apricot, walnut and almond. All were grown within a 20 mile radius. Now, due to changing farm economics, the almonds are king and the others pretty much just a memory. Actually English walnut isn't that great a firewood, you get a nice crackling fire for 20 minutes and end up with a huge batch of ashes. Almond and oak are probably the two favorite firewoods in California. They burn hot, leave a great bed of coals and last long enough that you're not getting up every 15 minutes to feed the fire.

OK, assuming you decide to begin cutting your own wood, where do you start? First you'll need at least one chainsaw, preferably two or three. Visit your local saw shop or hardware store for advice. Like everything else, when you're out in the field woodcutting, Murphy's Law is still in effect. Whatever can go wrong, will go wrong. Saws will get dull, the chains will jump off the bar, you need to refuel them regularly, etc. That's one of the reasons for multiple saws. Another is that you use different saws for different purposes. I believe that the ideal set up is a 24 inch saw for felling and cutting big trunks and limbs, an 18 inch saw for most cutting, and a little 16 incher for trimming and brushing.

If you have to use just one saw, the 18 inch bar is probably as good a compromise as any. With three saws and assorted paraphernalia don't expect to make any money cutting wood your first season. If you burn 3 to 4 cords a year, you'll probably just break even the first year. After that you'll probably realize significant savings every year by cutting your own.

Once you get your equipment, then you have to find a source of wood. In Northern California we have two primary wood sources; local orchards, and the National Forests. Both require a little planning. Odd as it may seem, most farmers, including orchardists, are actually in business to make a profit. During the life of an orchard, trees will blow down in storms, become sick, and eventually reach the point where they are no longer economically productive. A large orchardist will regularly be removing trees. They realize that even dead trees have value as fire wood and if you want to obtain a reliable wood source in local orchards, you'll either have pay a fee, or work out a sweat equity where you cut the trees and give the orchardist a portion of the wood in lieu of cash. It can be a fair deal for both parties.

The second main source of firewood is the National Forest Service which has a regular wood cutting program as part of the muli-use concept. Last time I heard, there were two kinds of wood cutting permits, a general non-specific permit to cut trees that are both dead and downed in the National forest, and a specific plot that is yours alone and has individual trees marked for removal. Contact the Forest Service for details. I always found the Forest Service easy to deal with. Naturally when cutting in the forest, you're going to get entirely different woods as a result. Pine, fir, oak and cedar are all plentiful at different areas of the forest.

Cedar is a great kindling and starter wood, it burns fast and hot. It makes a cheery, crackling fire and smells great, but doesn't last very long. It is relatively easy to start a fire with and burns reasonably long with good coals. Pine and fir are good mid-range woods that start fairly well and last reasonably long. If I could get only one variety of wood from the forest, I'd choose pine or fir. Oak is a little harder to start, but burns long and hot. You can put a couple chunks of oak on at bedtime and still have warmth in the morning. I love all the varieties of wood and mix them according to my mood.

Wood cutting isn't for everyone, but if you like to get some good physical exercise; it can be a great experience. You can make a family event of your woodcutting expeditions. Take a picnic lunch and get everyone involved. Everybody can do something, whether it's the actual cutting, loading the wood, keeping the saws running, or preparing the food. You'll be spending time outdoors and can enjoy the sight of hawks and eagles soaring overhead, or squirrels scampering through the forest. You can heat your home and save money doing it, while spending quality time with your family. This time next winter you can be curled up next to a cozy fire with a hot drink and a good book. It's a great benefit of being an outdoors addict.

⌘ ⌘ ⌘

THE BUZZARD ROOST

January 2007

Several months ago I stopped by my mom's house along about dusk. I was talking to Mom out in her driveway when a large shadow briefly blocked out the setting sun. I looked up and saw a large buzzard drift into a front yard tree. I really never expected to see a buzzard in the middle of town. Upon closer inspection I saw that the tree was loaded with buzzards. Heck, there must have been 25 or 30 of them. Since Mom is in her mid 80s I kidded that the buzzards must be waiting there for her. Mom laughed and agreed that she'd have to be more careful.

Last week I was at Mom's, chatting with my brother-in-law, Wes Huffman, and sure enough, the buzzards began to silently arrive, one by one. Although they are an integral part of nature, having a buzzard roost in your front yard is no picnic. A few dozen buzzards can really foul up the paint job on your car. In addition, a lot of folks just get a creepy sort of feeling with a flock of vultures 50 feet above them.

As humanity continues to expand, there are more and more incidents of us interacting with wild critters. Just night before last, my two dogs started barking up a storm and wouldn't stop. Much to my surprise, they had a possum cornered by the wood pile. The dogs were merrily barking and growling, and the possum was snarling back. After restraining the dogs I shooed the possum along down the fenceline to quieter pastures. I had to lock the darned dogs in the garage til morning to get any sleep.

It could just be my imagination, but it seems as though more and more now we're seeing wild critters in urban environs.

For the most part, I enjoy wildlife encounters. I love walking through my nearby park and seeing wild turkey or grey squirrels. Last winter in a driving rain I saw a coyote slogging through the volleyball pits. About a month ago, I pulled into a park to check my phone messages and watched a grey fox trot down the road at 10:00 in the morning. It was pretty cool! That fox just ignored me as though I wasn't even there.

Not all wildlife encounters are so benign, in Escalon a couple years ago a lady went to investigate the stories her grandkids were telling of a big cat growling at them from the corner of her garage. Sure enough, there was a full grown cougar. The woman called police and the cat was chased off. Its pretty scary thinking about what that cat might have done to her grandkids.

The litany goes on and on. Last week, local TV stations carried the footage of a black bear that walked in the front door of Barton Hospital in South Lake Tahoe. After looking around for a second two the bear left and went on about his business. Over the past 20 years or so I have put my Havahart Live Trap to good use. When the trap is sprung the critter gets caught in a cage and you can move him to a more remote area. I have caught and released about a dozen coons, a dozen possums, two foxes, and one spotted skunk. I'll tell you what, letting a skunk out of a livetrap without getting sprayed is impossible. My family made me sleep in the garage for a week.

Urban wildlife encounters are not always sweetness and light. Several years ago my cat was so severely mauled by a raccoon that I had to take him to the vet to be euthanized. Once wild critters get accustomed to mooching a free meal of catfood or dogfood they will keep coming back forever. To avoid having to kill neighborhood coons, or having your pets killed, be sure to store your pet food in tight critter-proof containers. Preventing the problem is a much better solution. I really enjoy seeing our wild neighbors but don't want to feed them and create a hazardous situation.

⌘ ⌘ ⌘

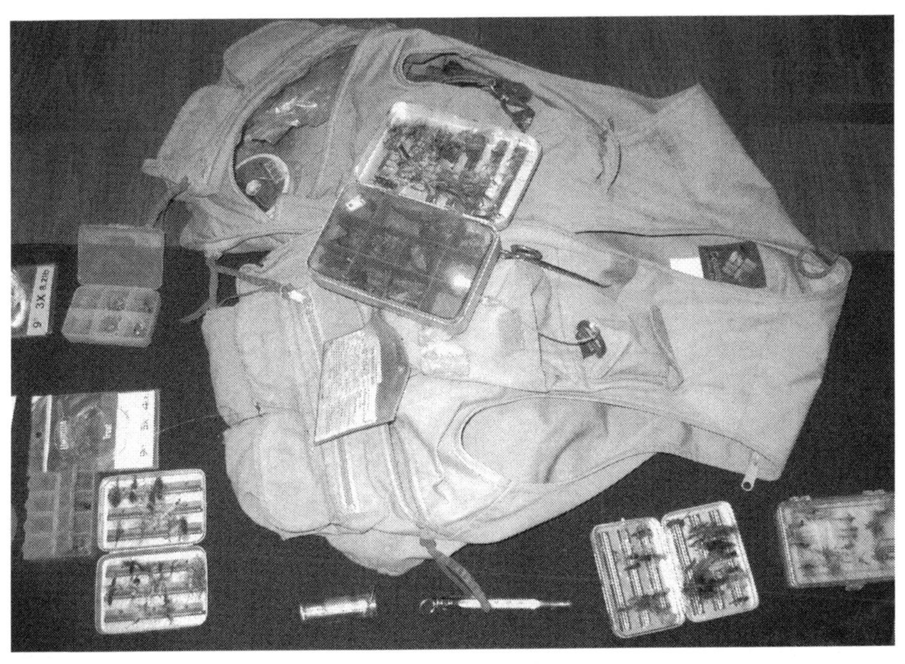

The Indispensable Fishing Vest

FISHING VEST PANIC

June 2008

A couple weeks ago I was up in the Sierra trout fishing with my son-in-law. At the end of the day, I dropped Jonathan off at his home, he unloaded his stuff, and we said our good byes. Last Friday, I was getting ready to go fishing with my son, Bo. I went out to the truck to get my fishing vest, and it wasn't there. I looked around the garage, no vest. Looked upstairs in the closet, no vest. I was beginning to panic; I couldn't find my fishing vest anywhere! This could be a major catastrophe. What would I do without my vest? Finally I found it hidden behind some furniture we had recently stored in the garage. Thank God!

I would be quite lost without my faithful fishing vest. During my anxiety prior to finding the vest, I began to wonder if it had perhaps been stolen from the back of my truck, or if I had laid it on the back bumper and driven off to have it fall into the road and be lost forever. Did I have insurance to cover a lost fishing vest? Would it be covered by my auto policy or maybe my homeowner's policy? Panic is a terrible thing. Boy was I relieved when I found my vest. What my scare did teach me, however, was that if my vest were lost, I would have no way of proving exactly what was in it so that I could make an insurance claim.

Now I can rest easy; I just finished an inventory of my fishing vest. It's amazing how much stuff one simple vest can hold. Among the stuff I carry astream in my vest are:

3 fly reels @ $220.00 each	$660
3 fly lines @ $59.00 each	$177
40 wet flies	$139

24 midges	$ 48
26 nymphs	$111
15 shad and panfish flies	$ 59
19 dry flies	$ 61
64 bass and salt water flies	$248

Among the other items I carry are, a landing net, a rain poncho, space blanket, hemostats, a Marbles Match Safe that keeps my matches dry, snakebite kit, sewing kit, stream thermometer, split shot, extra eyeglasses, suture kit, a leather and rubber leader straightener, a combination scale and measuring tape, assorted leaders, a Big Hunk candy bar, a bag of beef jerky, a sharpening stone, a buck folding hunter knife, an anglers clip, a fish counter, and a mesh drawstring collection bag.

While the above list seems like a lot of needless junk, I have been stuck out overnight in the wilderness, and those items come in really handy in making an overnight stay more comfortable. One of my buddies inadvertently spent a night alone along the McCloud River. He happened upon a large rattlesnake and was so startled that he fell and broke his leg. Poor Terry spent a miserable night lying in a trail until someone found him the following morning.

Back when I was a lot younger and dumber, I was so focused on following a fresh bear track in the Merced River Canyon, that I found myself over 10 miles from my camp when darkness fell. Because of all the stuff I carry, I was actually reasonably comfortable that night. I was warm, dry, and reasonably well fed. The next morning I awoke and hiked back to camp none the worse for wear.

Your fishing vest is much more than a carry all for fishing gear. It is your survival kit, your first aid kit, and your home away from home. Take care of your vest, and restock the supplies as you use them, and most importantly inventory its contents so that if you lose it, you will at least have a starting place to begin replacing it.

While it sounds sort of removed from fishing, see your insurance agent to make you're properly insured if you should be unfortunate enough lose your fishing vest. At least then, you'll have the peace of mind to enjoy your fishing.

⌘ ⌘ ⌘

REMEMBER GUN CASES?

August 2008

I believe that *Stand by Me* was one of the best coming of age movies of all time. It is a story of 4 boys who, in a journey seeking the body of a dead classmate, discover themselves. At the end of the film, one of the boys makes the observation that while one of their number will be groomed for greater things, most of them will be sent to shop class where they will make ash trays and birdhouses. I don't know if it's still the case, but when I went through junior high, boys took shop class and girls took home economics. We didn't have a choice; that's just how it was.

In shop class, each of us had to select and build a project that was a large part of our final grade. Some guys chose to build a hope chest; others designed and built fancy chess boards, or cabinets for the home. One guy even built a racing hydroplane. A handful of us chose to design and build our own gun cases. At the end of the year all the projects were put on display for the school open house. Some of the projects were beautiful works of art, some were functional furniture, and some were less than stellar.

I was pretty proud of my gun case. It held 7 guns: 6 slots for traditional rifles or shotguns, and a seventh slot, made extra-wide for a side-by-side, double- barrel shotgun. My gun case graced the bedroom I shared with my brother and had drawers underneath to store ammunition, gun cleaning stuff and related items. When I got married, my shop-project gun case became part of the furnishing of our new household. I guess it was as inevitable as rivers flowing to the sea, but somewhere along the line, something changed.

One year as a birthday gift, my wife bought me a fancy new glass-doored gun case and the old one got relegated to junk storage in the garage. Eventually, even the fancy glass gun case got replaced by a massive fire-proof gun safe that would still be intact after your house burned to the ground. Somewhere along the way my old shop project gun case faded away never to be seen again.

Of course, I rest easy at night knowing that my guns are safe from theft, flood, or fire. But I miss being able to enter my den and see my guns on display. It's true that guns stored in a controlled environment are protected from rust, dust and cobwebs, but I miss the sight of polished woodwork and inlaid metal and the smell of Hoppes #9.

About 20 years ago I attended a fundraiser at the house of a world traveling hunter. Old Bob surely invested more in his game room than I had in my entire house. Magnificent oak gun cases with lead glass doors and recessed ceiling lighting lined the north wall. From the east, a mounted leopard had leapt into a tree with a gazelle in his jaws and glared down at you, daring you to challenge him, while on the south a jackal waited for his chance to steal a meal from the leopard. Although Old Bob has gone on to that great safari in the sky, I wonder what became of his game room.

In 1965 a drive through the high school parking lot anywhere in the Central Valley would turn up several dozen pickups equipped with gun racks mounted in the cabs back window. Frequently there was both a shotgun and a rifle ensconced in the gun rack. During hunting season, many of us would hunt before or after class. Heck, I even remember what a treat it was to go shooting with our high school speech teacher. Boy, could he shoot a shotgun! Now, a gun in a vehicle at a local high school would probably produce a response from the local SWAT team. I know that our guns are safer in their gun vaults, and that we can't have pickups equipped with guns in the high school parking lot anymore, but sometimes, I think that maybe we were safer then than we are now. I miss my old gun case.

⌘ ⌘ ⌘

THE OBAMA EFFECT

May 2009

Stopped by a friend's house the other day to visit, and he gave me a bag full of old ammunition that had been lying around for 25 or 30 years. The ammo was a little dusty, but probably still good. The bag had about 10 pounds of assorted ammunition. It was almost like Christmas. The shells were coated with decades of dust but it looked as thought it was all still shootable ammo.

When I got home I began to sort and clean the ammo. There were 22 hollow points and solids, 38 special in wad cutters for target shooting, ball ammo and hollow points, and 357 magnum in snake shot, target, hunting, and defense bullets. All told there were about 250 rounds of assorted handgun ammunition. I had really hit the Mother Lode. The cost of ammunition has risen dramatically in the recent past and I was curious just how much my new treasure would retail for. A day or so later, I spotted the Bass Pro shop from the freeway and pulled in to check out their ammo prices. If you haven't been there yet, Bass Pro is like Disneyland for outdoor fanatics, they have so much stuff it'll knock your socks off.

Today however I was on a mission, I blew right past the fly shop, boat displays, and camouflage recliners, and headed straight for the gun department. Not being a stranger there, I rounded the corner for the ammo aisle and was shocked when I got there. It looked like a toy store on the day after Christmas! I was looking at row after row of almost completely empty shelves. Except for a couple boxes of oddball European calibers, and some specialty Cowboy Action 45 rounds, the shelves were completely bare. I asked the clerk what the problem was and she replied, "Obama." Inquiring further, I discovered that President Obama is jokingly referred to by the NRA as "The Gun Salesman of the Year."

I asked if Bass Pro had more ammo on order and the clerk replied, "Yes, but it won't make it to the shelves." I shouldn't have been so shocked when I was informed that word of an impending ammo shipment was passed like wildfire. As soon as a shipment of ammo arrives it is loaded on a cart and the clerk heads for the proper shelves. The clerk explained, "The customers are waiting like circling buzzards. They grab the ammo off the cart and head straight for the register." I figured that the Bass Pro clerk was just having a little fun with me, so I headed for a specialty gun shop. I knew they would have ammo up the ying yang. Guess what? Same story at the gun shop, empty shelves and the clerks were hoping to get more, but not holding their breaths. "Haven't you heard?" asked the clerk, "Everyone is scared spitless that Obama and his buddies in Congress are trying to outlaw ammunition."

I got an email joke the other day about a fellow who asked his stock broker what was the smart buy for the future. The Broker replied, "Canned goods and ammunition." Apparently the email is only partly a joke. A few days later I read in a front page newspaper article, that millions of Americans are so worried about the economy that they are stockpiling not just guns and ammo, but rice, beans, flour, bottled water and any other staples they can get in their closets and garages. Back at the gun shop, I figured that since ammo was in short supply, I would pick up a few extra boxes of primers and a couple extra cans of gunpowder. Wrong again, empty shelves and a shortage of reloading components.

Although I wasn't a supporter of President Obama, I figure he's my President and it's my country, so I wish him the best of luck. I really hope he can get the country moving again and stave off a depression. I'd love to see home sales pick up again and employers begin hiring again. But in the meantime a lot of Americans may have to rely on their old deer rifle to put meat on the table this winter. Whether we like it or not, the Obama Effect is real.

⌘ ⌘ ⌘

THE BILL OF RIGHTS

March 2010

Last week, the U.S. Supreme Court heard arguments on a case called McDonald v Chicago, which will most likely have an impact on you and your rights. Although the case focuses on the Second Amendment and your right to keep and bear arms, it appears to me to be much broader than that. It seems to me that the entire Bill of Rights may be at stake.

As you probably recall from your school days, the Bill of Rights is the first 10 amendments to the U.S. Constitution. They might sound familiar—the First Amendment guarantees us freedom of speech, freedom of the press, freedom of religion, and the right to peaceably assemble and petition our government. The Second Amendment gives the right to keep and bear arms; the Fourth Amendment protects us from unreasonable searches and seizures by the government, while the Fifth Amendment guarantees us due process of law. That's pretty important stuff. How important? You decide.

In 1769 the famous jurist William Blackstone wrote in his *Commentaries on the Laws of England*, that Catholics who were convicted of not attending the Church of England suffered certain penalties. Can you imagine that? You could be a criminal by belonging to the wrong church! Not good. The Bill of Rights guarantees us that such things cannot happen here in the United States. Sure different states have different preferences and traditions, but as Americans we have basic rights that no one can take away from us. In Boston, many people are Catholic, in Memphis there are a lot of Baptists, and in Skokie the majority may be Jewish, but as

Americans the Bill of Rights gives us the choice to belong to any church we wish. Until now.

In order to understand what is at stake here, a little background is in order. The City of Washington, D.C., had a law banning handgun ownership by its citizens. Dick Heller was a police officer in D.C. assigned to the Federal Judicial Center and carried a handgun everyday as part of his job. Heller decided he wanted to keep a handgun at his D.C. home for protection, and applied for a permit to do so. He was denied the right to have a gun and filed suit alleging that his constitutional rights were being violated. Eventually the case of District of Columbia v Heller worked its way all the way to the U.S. Supreme Court and in June of 2008 the Supreme Court issued its ruling. The court declared that the Second Amendment does indeed protect Dick Heller's right **as an individual** to keep and bear arms and struck down the District of Columbia gun ban.

Gun owners all over America celebrated this victory for the common citizen. There were similar gun bans in New York, San Francisco, and Chicago that would all be overturned. But wait! The City of Chicago doesn't see it that way. Can you believe that? Just last week, Chicago's lawyers argued that the Heller Decision and the Bill of Rights don't apply in Chicago. Otis McDonald, a retired maintenance engineer and Army Veteran applied for a gun permit in Chicago and was denied. Like Dick Heller, Otis Mc Donald filed suit to exercise his constitutional right to protect himself, and now it's in the hands of the Supreme Court. A decision is expected in the next few months. Hopefully, the court will decide that the Bill of Rights does indeed apply in Chicago as well as San Francisco and New York. If not, will we soon have to worry about getting busted for belonging to the wrong church?

⌘ ⌘ ⌘

Section Eight
PHILOSOPHY

THE FAYE TOAL THEORY OF ANGLING

October 1981

I was talking to a lady last weekend who told me that fishing was very much like playing slot machines. Instead of putting in a quarter, you put in your bait and hope for good luck. More often than not, so her theory goes, you lose, and when you do finally get lucky it's usually only in a rather modest way, It's the hope of hitting that big jackpot, or in the case of angling, catching that 10 pounder, that keeps you coming back for more.

The more I ponder the Faye Toal Theory of Angling, the more validity I see in it. Obviously, a sane person doesn't really expect to make money consistently playing slot, machines, it's much more practical to put your money in a bank. Fishing is very similar in that it's recreation we're after, not meat. If we were really after fish flesh it would undoubtedly be cheaper to buy it in the market, Just as playing slot machines is a whole lot more fun than visiting your local banker, so angling is a lot more fun than a visit to the fish market, And just as Casinos throw in lots of "extras," so there are other benefits to fishing besides fish.

One day a couple of years ago, I was out catfishing with Ray McCray and my dog stuck her head into the water and brought up a perfectly good fishing rod. I explained that if hunters could train dogs to retrieve ducks, I figured I could teach my dog to fetch fishing rods. Other useful stuff I've found while fishing includes knives, nets, boxes of trout flies, and skinny dippers. I've done a lot of trout fishing in the Mother Lode country and the amount of old relics I've amassed would fill a garage. My tool shed is stocked with axes, shovels, picks, and pry bars I've found astream.

Other finds have included: gold pans, cast iron stoves, a live trap, and even a capstan from a lumber mill. It's been a long time since I've found an old dynamite box that was still intact. I was always impressed with the workmanship of the dovetailed box corners and the boxes always had such expressive names like Hercules and Atlas. Time is beginning to take its toll, though, and I guess the only place you'd find such boxes anymore would be in a sheltered place like a mine tunnel or an old mine shack.

The amount of historical knowledge one can gain while fishing areas such as the Mother Lode is astounding. I learned about old bottle making processes from antique bottles found along the rivers. I still have an old soda bottle from the San Francisco Soda Works that had a rubber and wire stopper instead of today's bottle caps. I learned some basic hydraulics when my father and I found a hydraulic ram used to lift water for mining and irrigation purposes.

I've picked up a lot of knowledge about Indians while finding arrowheads, beads, and mortars and pestles. No doubt about it, keeping one's eyes open while fishing can provide more meaningful history lessons than a classroom lecture. The larger relics one finds can really amount to work and even pain just to get them home. Once I found an old safe with the door blown off. It took five people to try to load it in the truck.

Angling has always been a learning experience to me, but through fishing, I've learned enough to make my old history teacher proud. The next time you are out fishing, especially if it's with kids, keep your eyes open and you'll learn about a lot more than just fish. Besides, next time you and the kids are heading out the door to go fishing (without having cut the lawn first), you can always tell your spouse, "But dear, I was just doing this for the kids."

⌘ ⌘ ⌘

THE SINS OF THE FATHERS

March 1982

Early last week, I was about to leave one stuffy meeting and go to another one a few blocks away. On a whim, I decided to walk rather than drive. I could sure use the exercise, and the fresh air might help clear the cobwebs out of my mind. On any ordinary day that would be a perfectly logical idea, but on this particular day it was pouring down rain. I walked across the bridge at the head of the Stockton Channel and caught the full force of the wind-driven rain as it whipped over the whitecaps. I was suddenly laughing at myself because I was actually enjoying the experience. Would any sane person enjoy being lashed by a storm?

I guess I can't help it; I'm incurably hooked on the outdoors. While fishing is my favorite excuse for being outdoors, it doesn't really matter, as long as I'm out enjoying Mother Nature. Last winter, I was up in the mountains cutting firewood with a friend. We worked steadily, cutting, splitting, and loading the wood. By the end of the day, I had aches where I didn't know I had muscles. Still, it was a great time. I sometimes ask myself why an otherwise normal person would submit to muscle cramps, storms, poison oak, rattlesnakes, and falling off cliffs. I guess it's all my dad's fault.

As far back as I can remember, we were outdoors enjoying nature. As toddlers, Dad would take my brother and sister and me out to Oak Island, and we'd catch a whole washtub full of catfish and bluegills. Then we'd bring em home alive and keep them in a backyard wading pool all summer. On summer evenings we'd sit in lawn chairs with our feet in the wading pool and play with our pet fish. Did you know that by stroking catfish on the belly with your fingers, you can hypnotize them so they roll over and float belly up? It's true! I've done it.

I must have been about 8 years old when I saw my first live rattlesnake and about 11 when I killed my first rattler with my BB gun. At about age 10, Dad took my brother and me out into the hills South of Tracy when we came across a confrontation between a rattler and a roadrunner. We sat mesmerized for almost an hour watching that rattler strike at the bird and the roadrunner dart around the snake and peck with amazing speed. Eventually the roadrunner won and the rattler became his dinner. It was amazing to watch. The only roadrunner most kids see is on TV being chased by a coyote. The poor kids don't even know what they're missing. Seeing the real thing is incredible.

For some reason, I love storms. Lord, I love storms. I suspect that's because I got trapped by a storm for an entire afternoon with a beautiful young lady. That may well have been the best storm of my life. One winter I was about halfway across a frozen Lake Alpine when the ice began to crack all around me. I learned more about prayer in ten minutes than in an entire year of perfect attendance at church. I also learned not to go out on a frozen lake without checking the ice thickness.

What's all this got to do with writing an outdoor column? Maybe to serve as a warning to those of you with children and grandkids. If you're not careful, your young ones could get hooked on the outdoors too. The next time you see some simple soul wandering aimlessly in the rain with glazed eyes, just remember, it could happen to you!

⌘ ⌘ ⌘

OPENING DAY MAGIC

April 1982

There is a certain magic which accompanies the opening day of trout season. In and of itself, there would seem to be nothing particularly outstanding about the last Saturday in April. As often as not, it's raining, snowing, or downright cold and miserable. Not only that, the fishing is very hit and miss, being either very good or terrible. I suspect the real magic of opening day lies in the anticipation of things to come. While the weather may actually be cold and wretched, one is comforted by the thought of the warming rays of sunny days yet unborn.

Now, as opening day gets closer, my anticipation level builds. I find myself checking and rechecking my gear. I've set up my fly tying kit in the living room and tie trout flies as I watch the evening news. I go through my fishing vest and replace the items consumed or lost during the past season. I come across my angling log book and replace the scribbled pages with new ones waiting to be written upon. I read the old entries in my log before placing them with their counterparts of years past.

I am reminded of fish that got away and of fish that didn't. There was a giant rainbow on the Tuolumne that snapped my leader just before I could net him. The same year, 20 miles further upstream there was another rainbow just as big, who broke my leader just after I netted him. I think of the huge rattler, as big around as my arm, who became dinner for two, and I also think of the tiny little rattler who almost ended my career as an angler in the bottom of the Merced River canyon.

I can almost see the bald eagle that flew just over my head in the Stanislaus canyon, and I can almost hear the sound of the flock of wild turkey I flushed along the Mokelumne. I remember the hair standing up on the back of my neck as I watched little wisps of steam rising from a pile of bear dung. I recall my prayer of gratitude for the poison oak bush I was able to grab to prevent me from falling off a 50 foot cliff. I can laugh now, in retrospect, at how funny I must have looked as I and my brand new Pinto floated down a creek I was trying to ford. Of course, it didn't seem very funny at the time as the water was rushing in filling up my new car. Nor did it seem especially hilarious at the time when I stepped on a hornets nest and had to jump into the river to escape them.

The shoe was on the other foot when Chuck Raffety got washed over a waterfall, I worried like mad until he came up swimming and then I began to laugh. I can still picture old Frank Adams in the pith helmet he used to wear, and Carl Upton cooking breakfast on the louvered hood scrounged from an abandoned Model A.

This weekend, I'll be out taking my chances along with two million other anglers. I really don't know whether I'll be catching lots of fish under blue skies or if I'll get snowed out and catch no fish at all. But I do know that this opening day holds the promise of angling memories to come. I've also got a pretty good hunch that as long as there are anglers and opening days, the magic will always be the same.

⌘ ⌘ ⌘

GIVE A BIG MACK FOR CHRISTMAS

December 1982

It's almost too late to buy any more Christmas gifts now, but I'd like to share with you an idea for a gift for someone that you hold very dear. It's best suited for kids, but it also suitable for spouses, best friends, or anyone you really care for. I began to fish when I was quite young. In fact, I was so young that I don't remember when I caught my first fish, or when I got my first fishing rod.

But I do remember Big Mack. Big Mack was not a hamburger, but rather, an incredible trout that lived in a tremendous pool in a crystal clear trout stream. There was a huge boulder as big as a house on the west bank of Big Mack's pool. A giant oak tree grew out of a crack in the boulder and shaded most of the pool in the afternoon.

Big Mack was a huge Rainbow Trout who made his home in the deep sheltered water at the foot of the boulder. I remember how Dad would teach my brother and me to be extremely careful as we approached his pool. We'd begin our stalk over a hundred yards away and stay low and far back from the water so he couldn't see us.

Ever so carefully, we'd inch our way out onto the boulder, under the oak tree, and peer cautiously over the edge and down into the water. Seeing Big Mack was almost like seeing a ghost. At first, there was nothing but clear water and a rocky bottom. Suddenly, as if out of nowhere, he would materialize in the current. "Careful now!" Dad would whisper. "If we make just one sudden move, he'll vanish as quickly as he appeared."

I remember watching Dad as he'd strip line off the reel and make a false cast with his fly rod, then another, and another, until he had just the right amount of line out. Then came the cast and the fly would drift gently down and land near the head of the pool and drift along the edge of the current toward the base of the boulder. Watching Big Mack rise to the fly was like watching an instant replay in slow motion. He came up out of the depths, and up and up, until you could see the white of his mouth as he engulfed the fly.

Then, he'd head leisurely back down until he felt the pull of the line. Back up he'd race and make a tremendous leap out of the water so that his body would fall on the tight line and break it. If you were quick enough to lower your rod tip and put some slack in the line, you might keep him on long enough to see three or four of those incredible leaps. Sooner or later, though, the leader would break, or he'd throw the hook. Then he'd vanish down into the depths from whence he came.

Every time we lost Big Mack, Dad would say something like "Oh well, he puts up such a great fight, and he's such a magnificent fish, that I'd probably release him anyway, so that I could come back and fish for him again."

As we got older, my brother and I would try our luck on Big Mack. The story was always the same, the cautious stalk, the cast, the slow-motion rise, the incredible leaps, and then an empty line and a vanished ghost. Although we never caught Big Mack, we learned techniques, like a careful stalk or dropping your rod tip to create slack. We learned about fish behavior, and trout habitat. Most importantly, we learned values like sportsmanship, and reverence and appreciation of God's creatures and the natural world they lived in.

When I reminisce back to Christmas' past, I think not of bikes which have long since turned to rust, nor of toys broken and discarded long ago. When I remember Christmas, I remember a new fishing rod, or the double barreled shotgun I received on my thirteenth Christmas, or the engraved knife I received on my twenty-fifth Christmas. I remember these things because of the time my parents invested in me to teach me how to use them properly.

This year you may want to consider giving your child or other loved one a fishing rod, or rifle, or camera, or paints and brushes that they can use in the outdoors. Use these gifts as a catalyst to set aside the time to be with your children and instruct them in their proper use, their history, and the values that they should represent. The material gifts will rust and wear out, but the intangible gifts such as the time you spent with your children, the values you taught them, and the love you gave them, are gifts that will never die. McDonald's makes a fine hamburger, but my Big Mack will last forever.

Merry Christmas and Tight Lines!

⌘ ⌘ ⌘

FATHER'S DAY REFLECTIONS

June 1983

It's hard to believe, but I've been writing this column for almost exactly 30 years now. A lot of fishing and hunting seasons have come and gone. But a theme that has pretty consistently run through my observations has been all of the values I learned from my parents. As the old saying goes, "When I was 17 my dad was pretty dumb, but as I got older, Dad got smarter."

A decade or so ago I wrote a column for Father's Day that suggested you give Dad an outdoor gift that would put you afield with him when he used it. I have a lot of great outdoor gifts that my Dad gave me over the years, a custom made pocket knife, my first 22 rifle at age 12, my first shotgun at 13, and a 357 revolver when I graduated college. Interestingly it isn't the gifts that hold the value, but rather the memories of the times he spent teaching me to use them.

This Father's Day, if your dad is still alive, rejoice in your good fortune, and take him outdoors for some quality time together. If you can hunt or fish together, great. Even if old dad can't get up the hills like he used to, you can go to Yosemite and have lunch at the Ahwanee together, or visit one of the many fine Delta restaurants and watch the sun set on the water.

Enjoy old dad while you can. Even though he may seem eternal. Trust me, he's not. Little did I know decades ago, that one day my old dad wouldn't be around for me to reciprocate. While I can no longer go fishing with Dad ever again, if I take my son fishing, or shooting, I can help pass on some of the values Dad gave to me.

Recently I've been noticing all of the advertising in the newspapers and on TV aimed at selling all sorts of Father's Day gifts. There are some great gifts to be had out there and I wish all the merchants well, but nonetheless, I sometimes think that we are placing too much emphasis on the material aspects and too little emphasis on the fact that Father's Day ought to be a celebration of how much we appreciate our fathers.

If your father, or husband, is an angler, hunter, or outdoorsman of any sort, let me make a recommendation for a Father's Day gift. First buy him a material sort of gift that pertains to his favorite outdoor pastime, a fishing rod, new hunting vest, binoculars, you get the idea . Then give him the important gift, the one that no one can give to him but you, offer to take him out to use his new possession for the first time, or in the case of you wives, give him a hand written weekend pass, exempting him from all household chores for the weekend of his choice, so that he can get out and enjoy his outdoor sport. Offer to accompany him if he wishes, or for you to stay at home with the kids is what he would prefer.

What the heck, make it an annual tradition, Every Father's Day he gets a weekend pass. Such traditions are the glue that holds families together. When I was a kid, we had nursed an injured hawk back to health and had grown quite fond of him. Dad insisted that we let the hawk go free, even though we would never see him again. Dad told us that the greatest gift one could give was freedom, even if it hurt to give it. I don't think that I'll ever forget the sight of that hawk as he soared away over the oaks to freedom. Make this Father's Day one that he'll never forget. Give him the gift of yourself.

⌘ ⌘ ⌘

FISHING PARTNERS

August 1983

I started looking through my copy of Bartlett's Quotations some time ago to find an appropriate comment about the nature of friendship. It turns out old Ralph Waldo Emerson; pretty well hit the nail on the head about a hundred years ago when he observed "A friend may well be reckoned the masterpiece of nature." While that is true about friendship in general, it's especially true for anglers.

It really doesn't matter whether you love to drift a valley river tossing spinner baits for bass, fly fish a high mountain meadow for trout, or troll for trophy marlin off Cabo San Lucas, there are really very few people out there who are ideally suited to fish with you or me. I'm sure you're not as eccentric as I am, but I have a few odd habits that make it almost impossible to find someone well suited to fish with me. Thus, finding a good fishing partner is truly like finding Emerson's "Masterpiece of Nature."

Most folks who've fished with me will swear that I run up the stream. I figure it's my Dad's fault because that's how he taught me. I give each pool, or other likely looking spot, about three casts, and then I move on. I reckon that if they don't hit my fly by the third cast, I must have spooked them.

Most normal anglers spend what seems like ten minutes on each pool. While I tell a new fishing companion to fish his pool, then walk around me to the pool above, it rarely works because they just fish too darned slow, (or I fish too fast). Thus it's a pleasure to find someone who fishes at the same speed as me. We can hopscotch around each other all day and neither feels guilty about leaving the other behind or angry at being left behind. We can stop to eat lunch together and philosophize on the nature of life.

Another quirk of mine is the reason why I fish. I fish purely for relaxation, that's all. Oftentimes, I'll fish all day, catch dozens of fish and take none home because I released them all. Other times, I've fished all day and caught nothing at all, but considered the trip a great success because we saw a mountain lion, or a bear or a bald eagle.

I gauge the success of my angling expeditions by the absence of a knot in my shoulders, by not having heard a telephone ring all day, or by thrill I got when a big one got away. In my mixed up value system, watching a kingfisher dive into a stream to catch a trout or watching a bear tear apart an old rotten log for the grubs inside is far more valuable than putting hatchery trout on a stringer.

Perhaps one of the best reasons why a normal person shouldn't go fishing with me is my affinity for adventure. Hiking into a two thousand foot deep canyon in hundred degree heat may seem crazy to most folks, but it's like an engraved invitation to me. Think about it. If 99% of the people wouldn't be crazy enough to go into some God forsaken hole, then the fishing there ought to be fantastic. Right?

The uncertainty of whether an old jeep road will lead to angling paradise or piscatorial purgatory is the frosting on the cake for me. You never know, when setting out in search of rainbows in a chasm or Goldens in the high country whether you'll strike paydirt or a dry hole.

Heck, sometimes we don't even know if the car will get us there and back again. My friend, Rick Hodges, gives me a hard time about my occasional breakdowns, but don't let him kid you. He exaggerates all those stories about broken axles, batteries failing, tires blowouts, blown engines and the like. He does admit though, that we've had some great adventures.

Finding someone as crazy as I am is next to impossible. Even more difficult, is finding a partner whose spouse is tolerant of such craziness. Although are more accurate terms, this is a family oriented newspaper so the best way I can describe a lot of anglers is "henpecked." There ought to be a medal for those sainted fishing widows (and widowers) who are secure enough to let their spouses' fish as they wish. Thank you, Mary, for being an understanding spouse.

To find a companion who is so near oneself that, for the most part, conversation is unnecessary, is akin to finding a four leaf clover. To find someone who finds joy in losing a large fish, and beauty in a coiled rattler, is like finding a mirror to one's soul.

Experiences shared with such an angling companion are those seared indelibly into your memory, to be dredged up on rainy nights and savored, like brandy, before a winter fire. I raise my glass to you, that masterpiece of nature, the perfect fishing partner.

⌘ ⌘ ⌘

THANKSGIVING THOUGHTS

November 1983

When I first got the opportunity to write an outdoor column on a regular basis, I had two immediate thoughts; first, how lucky I was to be able to get paid to write about fishing and have it become tax deductible, and secondly how easy it would be to simply go out each week and then put something down on paper. Over the years I've learned that I was half right, I was, and am now, still lucky to be able to write about the outdoors I love so much.

I was wrong, however, about how easy it would be to come up with stories week in and week out. There are times when I sit down in front of my typewriter and absolutely nothing ends up on paper. Sometimes I go for a walk in the night air to clear my mind, sometimes I peruse my shelves of outdoor books for inspiration, while sometimes I put my mangy old fishing hat on, and sit back in my chair to conjure up outdoor thoughts.

Usually one or more of the above methods works, but once in a rare while, nothing seems to work. The last few days have been like that, no matter what I tried, no luck. As is often the case, the answer was right in front of me, but it took someone else to see it. My patient wife, Mary, after seeing me agonize for days, suggested, "Why don't you write about Thanksgiving from an outdoor perspective?" It was as though a floodgate had been opened; suddenly I had more things to write about than my editors would give me space for.

Probably more than any of the others, two specific thoughts stand out in relation to Thanksgiving and the outdoors. First is how it emphasizes the extent to which we are still dependent upon nature for our very survival, and secondly, the extent to which Thanksgiving has been a family oriented holiday.

Think about it. When you picture the pilgrims on the first Thanksgiving, don't you envision pilgrim hunters bringing a wild turkey or two into the settlement for the feast? Don't you just as readily picture a group of Indians bringing a deer carried on a pole?

As we become more and more urbanized, it becomes increasingly difficult for us to see how dependent we are on the whims of nature. For most of us, if we really wanted to, we could sit down to a plentiful meal at almost any time of the year. But to those first Americans, they could only experience the benefits of nature's bounty in the fall when the crops became ripe, and the game was getting fat in preparation for winter.

We, as anglers and hunters, are probably far more aware of our inextricable ties to nature than "normal" urban dwellers. Yet, at least once a year the rest of the populace gets a tiny bit of exposure that may help them to understand that we outdoors enthusiasts are simply seeking to be a small part of the natural scheme of things, and not that we are trying to destroy it. If Thanksgiving served no other purpose than to promote tolerance of the outdoor ethic, it would be a most valuable holiday indeed.

The family nature of Thanksgiving, is pretty well accepted by most. After all, when was the last time you went to a company Thanksgiving party? As is no doubt true for many families, Thanksgiving for me always provided an opportunity for family members to gather from far and wide on at least one day of the year, and maintain and re-establish old family ties.

I don't quite know how it evolved, but our family somehow developed a tradition of going outdoors in the late afternoon hours to work off the lethargy brought on by over-indulgence in assorted foods. One thing led to another, and before long, Thanksgiving afternoon turned into a family hunt. Usually it was duck season, and often times, pheasants were also fair game. Of course, there were always rabbits and squirrels to seek too. We'd head afield, a motley collection of young and old, Grandpa, and uncles, cousins, and all. If we were lucky, we would get a few shots and maybe even return with a pair of pheasants, some rabbits, and a duck or two for the pot.

Mostly what we got was a lot of camaraderie, and yet another retelling of Grandpa's hunting tales of years gone by. We all knew by heart the story of how Grandpa went out duck hunting with only two shotgun shells and returned with four ducks (or was it five). We all knew equally well, how Grandpa began tracking one bear in the snow and it was joined by another bear and another and yet another until Grandpa finally decided he didn't want to have to take on five bears with a single shot muzzle loader.

When I look back, I think that it was really immaterial how many creatures, if any, we brought home. What was important was that at least once a year we got to participate in a familial passing of traditions and values from one generation to another, and yet another.

I am grateful for a host of blessings, but especially that we have an opportunity that enables us to gather together and give thanks to our God, however we perceive him, for the blessings he has given us.

I don't know about you, but I'm thankful that we have the opportunity to fish in clean waters, and hunt for wild game. I'm thankful for all of the generations who have been able to pass along such traditions and who hopefully will be able to do so for many generations to come. It is my sincere hope that you, too, will have so much to be grateful for.

⌘ ⌘ ⌘

GIFTS THAT MATTER

December 1983

Last week, I came up with a few gift ideas for outdoor enthusiasts. I closed the column with the idea that the best gifts of all were those in which you give of yourself. While it's been reiterated countless times, the concept of giving of one's self never really gets outdated. While I'm admittedly biased, it seems to me that there are more opportunities for such giving if you enjoy the outdoors.

A recent ad on TV caught my attention as being one of the best I've seen in a long time. It's an ad in which a father's voice tells how all he used to see of his son was the back of his head in front of the TV, and how all the son saw of his dad was the top of his head protruding from behind the newspaper. The father goes on to say that ever since they got a pair of those wonderful atvs, both father and son have gone out riding almost every weekend. All the while, you are seeing exciting scenes of the father and son climbing hills, splashing through creeks, and racing through the woods. The dad concludes that he doesn't think his son really knows much about a generation gap, and come to think of it, neither does he. It's an absolutely great ad.

There are so many gifts that one can give which require only an expenditure of money, but the really great ones also require that you spend time with the recipient as he uses the gift. Those are the gifts that really matter. A perfect example is a gun, particularly a child's first gun.

When you give a 12 or 13 year old kid that first single shot 22 or 20 gauge there is an ethical requirement that you take the youngster afield and instruct him in it's safe use, and the common sense concepts like never killing more than he can eat, or why he shouldn't shoot hen pheasants.

If you're thinking about buying a kid a gun, but aren't going to be around to give him the proper guidance, then perhaps you'd better think again. Like most things in life, a gun can be a two—edged sword, it can be a source of family ties, education and communication that brings families closer together. A gun, if simply handed to a kid like any other toy, can bring senseless tragedy. The choice is yours, and I heartily recommend the former.

The situation is so very similar for lots of other items too. A dirt bike can be the best thing that ever happened to a kid if you go out riding with him, but it could lead to a lot of trouble and even serious injury or death if a kid is just turned loose with no supervision.

A simple thing like a pocket knife can be one of the world's most useful gifts, or it also has the potential for trouble if the recipient isn't mature enough or properly trained in its use. The ironic thing about giving gifts that will require an investment of your time is that the person who gets the most from the gift is often the one who gives it.

Years ago, I used to belong to Big Brothers of America, and one Christmas I gave my little brother, Billy, a fly rod. I taught Billy how to cast and how to tie his own flies, and finally the day came when Billy caught his very first trout on his own rod with a fly he tied himself. He was so proud I thought he was going to bust his buttons. But I don't think Billy even knew that I was even prouder of him than he was.

Over the years, I've learned a lot about giving, mostly from my parents but later on, from people who became close friends because they gave of themselves to me. One such friend was Okla Primm. Oak and I would go out to cut wood together and more often than not, he'd say "I've got more wood than I need at home Lad, why don't you take this load." Sometimes we'd be coming back into town with a truckload of firewood and Oak would ask, "Lad, you wouldn't mind if we stop by Widow Smith's house and give her this load of ours would you?" He'd give me a camp stove he said he no longer needed and then suggested we go up in the mountains camping so he could show me how to use it.

Yes indeed, I learned an awful lot about giving from Okla Primm. He died last week and was buried on Tuesday. One thing that wasn't buried with him was his spirit of giving. Memorials of granite and marble are all fine and dandy, but for my money the best kind of all are the ones that live on in the hearts of those to whom we've given.

People think about giving especially at this time of year, but once you get into the habit, it's a tough one to break. If you want to give a gift this Christmas that will last longer than any other, give one that requires an investment of your own time, and you'll have given a truly lifelong gift, a gift that truly matters.

⌘ ⌘ ⌘

GOD AND THE GREAT OUTDOORS

June 1988

If you are an atheist you're not going to agree with this column. Of course that's part of the beauty of our form of government, we can agree to disagree. The more time I spend enjoying the great outdoors, the more I become convinced that all that beauty and intricacy has to be the work of a Supreme Being. I find evidence everywhere of God's handiwork in the outdoors.

Without a doubt the most intense conversation I ever had with the Almighty was on the ice of a frozen lake in the late winter. I was walking across the ice when all of a sudden I heard sounds much like gunshots. I quickly deduced that it was the ice cracking under my weight. That was when I began to converse with the Lord in a big hurry, I promised that if He got me off that lake alive I would have perfect attendance in church for an entire year. Then the ice gave way beneath my feet and I began to drop into the icy water.

My salvation came a split second later when I hit another layer of ice underneath a layer of water. I have no idea how there could be a second layer of ice beneath the water, but there it was. When I got to shore with soaked and freezing feet, I was able to kindle a fire and thaw out. Sure enough, I never missed a single Sunday in church for a whole year. Hey, a deal is a deal.

Actually, if you have ever stood upon a coastal peak and seen the endless ocean, or stood atop a mountain peak and seen the snow covered mountains, you could not doubt the magnificence of His work. Try standing on the rim of the

Grand Canyon or looking up at the stars on a summer night and then tell me that it was just some giant accident.

I find beauty almost everywhere I look in the great outdoors. More importantly I find indisputable proof of everlasting life. Did you ever see the brilliant buds of the snow flower pushing up thru the springtime snow? He existed then, He exists now, and He always will.

To me, the great outdoors renews my spirit and recharges my batteries. Out there I find Cathedrals far more magnificent than any mortal can make. When I occasionally miss church on Sunday, I only feel a little guilty because to me there can be no greater evidence of God. Perhaps that's one reason why I spend so much time out there. Somehow I hear His voice more clearly in the midst of a trout stream than in church. You might want to give it a try, but do stay off the thin ice.

⌘ ⌘ ⌘

EPHEMERAL TROUT

March 1989

Late last Spring I had an experience that was exceedingly exciting and also exceedingly embarrassing. The incident occurred on a warm sunny day when Phil Hall and I were hiking into a small creek that feeds into one of the foothill reservoirs. I had told Phil that the week before I'd caught and released several trout from 16 to 20 inches long.

In addition to being a fishing fanatic Phil is also my minister, so we managed to find a day when we could sneak away. As we were approaching the stream we were walking through some old piles of dredger tailings left long ago by gold miners. Suddenly, as if out of nowhere, a giant rattler with an exceedingly nasty disposition was attempting to send me to the hereafter. In my excitement at trying to avoid an early demise, I cut loose with a stream of invectives that would have made a sailor blush. It was bad enough almost being nailed by a rattler, but swearing up a blue streak in front of your preacher is really embarrassing.

It's all because of my refusal to let go of those darned Ephemeral Trout. What a neat word! Ephemeral, according to my trusty Webster's Dictionary, means "lasting for only a day" or "lasting for only a short time." I discovered Ephemeral Trout quite by accident. My dad and I were driving to the Sierra for some early season trout fishing. We were passing by one of the many large foothill reservoirs, and as I looked over the cliff I spotted a nice looking little trout stream at the bottom of the canyon below. I asked Dad to pull over at the next wide spot for a better look. Dad thought I was crazy because the stream at the bottom went bone dry almost every summer.

Nonetheless, I was able to convince Dad that we ought to hike down and give it a try. When we got to the waters edge the stream was clear and cold. On about my 5th cast I hooked and landed a rainbow of about 16 inches from a pool that was knee deep and 30 feet wide. My dad and I only caught 3 trout each that day, but the first one was the smallest! That was the beginning of my addiction to Ephemeral Trout.

After a lot of trial and error, I finally began to figure out what was going on. These trout were spawners that would wait until the winter rains would swell the previously dry creek high enough for them to enter it and spawn in its abundant gravel beds. The big spawners lay their eggs in the cold, well oxygenated gravel of the creek in late winter, and then migrate back down into the deeper and safer waters of the lake. The eggs would hatch, and the tiny fry would live in the relative safety of the creek until the water temperatures began to rise as spring progressed into summer. Then the fingerlings would follow the path of their parents and also migrate down to the lake before the creek dried up each summer.

I discovered that I got lousy results immediately after the arrival of a big winter storm because the water was too cloudy for the fish to see my offerings. But by waiting about a week or ten days for the water levels to drop a little and the clarity to improve, the fishing was usually super. On the other hand, if you wait too long, the levels drop too much, and the warmer weather raises temperatures too high. Of course, as it gets warmer, you also increase the chances of finding one of the nasty critters that caused me so much excitement and embarrassment in front of my preacher.

By their very nature these ephemeral streams have limitations: they are usually small and thus cannot take much fishing pressure unless it's on a catch and release basis where you return all the fish unharmed back into the creek. Remember these fish are spawners and are going to provide for fishing in future years. If you don't mind a short drive, and are looking for a chance to catch some really nice sized trout, then perhaps these Ephemeral Trout might be just the ticket.

⌘ ⌘ ⌘

NEW YEAR'S OUTDOORS

January 2008

This is the time of year when folks sit down and think about New Year's resolutions. If you put some thought into the process, it can really be worthwhile. Stop and take inventory of yourself and pay special attention to things you haven't done. When most people look back on their lives, they regret not the things they've done, but rather the things they haven't done. The recent film, *The Bucket List,* starring Jack Nicholson and Morgan Freeman, is a pretty good example of that concept.

Ask yourself, "What things in the outdoors haven't I done?" Maybe you keep promising yourself that one of these days you're going to go fishing in Alaska. Hey! You're not getting any younger. DO it. Perhaps you keep thinking that you're going to take your family on a white water raft trip. Book It Now!

Think back on the truly memorable times in your life and resolve that this year you're going to do more of it. Remember the time you rented a houseboat on the Delta and fished and swam all day and played cards and partied all night? Book a houseboat at Lake Powell, or Shasta Lake. Heck, go whole hog and book a sailboat in the Caribbean! Life is too short not to experience it.

Your new outdoor adventures don't all have to be expensive trips to exotic locations. You can resolve to go catfishing more often with an old friend. Do it now while you're both still alive. I used to swear I was gonna hunt more quail with Coach Poletti, but he's gone now and I'll never see him nail 2 quail with one shot again. Take your kids or your grandkids out to a local creek and catch crawdads. They'll get wet and muddy, have a great time, and never forget it.

This year I'm going to backpack one more time into the wilderness with my son in search of the world's rarest trout. We may not catch any, but we're sure gonna try.

I suppose I could have a coronary out there in the wilds, but what the heck? At least I'd go out doing something I love. As far as I know, we only go through this life once, so before you finish, make sure that it's a worthwhile trip. Get out there and enjoy the outdoors while you can!

⌘ ⌘ ⌘

THE 90/10 RULE

October 2008

Everyone who fishes would love to discover that secret fishing hole that's just loaded with hungry fish waiting to attack your hook. It's equally true that everyone who hunts would love to find that secret spot that the biggest buck, or wild boar, or bull elk calls home. You may have heard the old rule of thumb that decrees that **10% of the hunters get 90% of the game** and that 10% of the anglers catch 90% of the fish. The other side of that rule means that 90% of the hunters and anglers get only 10% of the game and fish. Actually, there's a lot of truth to the 90/10 rule. The trick is learning how you can become one of the 10%.

Basically there are three factors which will determine if you going to be part of the 10% group or if you are content to remain in the 90%. The key ingredients to outdoor success are knowledge, dedication, and practice practice, practice. Let's say that you're determined to become a super trout fisher and regularly catch far more trout than anyone else.

These concepts could just as easily apply to bass fishing, steelheading, deer hunting, or any other outdoor pursuit. In order to become a better trout fisher you have to learn more, you have to try harder, and you have to put in longer hours.

In these days of DVD's and VCR's and online connectivity it's easier to learn than ever before. While obtaining outdoor knowledge on line or electronically is great, there are still some old fashioned ways that are darned effective too. There are an amazing number of books at your local library that will get you started and give you lots of invaluable outdoor knowledge.

Another great way to learn is to attend one of the many hunting or fishing clubs that abound in the area. The outdoor clubs are always looking for new members. They regularly have programs that will teach you fly tying, rod building, stream and lake techniques and even how to cook your catch. They have club outings where you can get out and actually try that new casting technique you've read about. Or you can have a fellow club member instruct you.

If you are a hunter, there are hunting clubs you can join in Stockton, Manteca, Escalon, and Oakdale. The National Rifle Association has great programs for shooters which will develop and hone your accuracy with your rifle. California Department of Fish and game holds regular classes open to the public will help you become more aware of the habits of deer, bear and wild hogs.

Another great source of information is the wide array of hunting and fishing clinics sponsored by the manufacturers of outdoor equipment. Bass Pro is in the midst of a series of such clinics right now.

All the outdoor education you absorb is great but the next factor is putting that knowledge into practice. Let's imagine a stretch of stream that has a heavy growth of streamside bushes on both sides. The current cuts along the far bank and the bushes hang down and almost touch the water. You know that there's likely to be a dandy Trout laying back under those overhanging branches. There's no room for a back cast because you'll get snagged in the bushes behind you. What do you do? Here's where the dedication and Practice, Practice, Practice, comes into play. You can sometimes use the roll cast to get your fly in there without getting snagged. If that doesn't work you can use the bow cast. Most of the time both casts are not really needed or even desirable. But in the right situation they can be the trick that saves the day.

The final factor that enters the equation is dedication. Practice that roll cast when you don't need to, and then do it again tomorrow, and again the next day. Before too long you'll be able to do it in your sleep. Heck, I catch some of my best trout in my sleep.

Another manifestation of dedication is that you want to succeed more than most other anglers. You are willing to walk a couple miles extra to get to the stretch of water that no one else fishes very often. You are willing to hike 2,000 feet down into that canyon and then the grueling 2,000 feet back up again at the days end. When the thunderheads begin to gather and the rain begins to pour down, the average guy will pack it in and quit but you pull out your poncho and have some of the best fishing of the year.

Oddly enough, once you get to the point where you can catch far more fish than the law allows, you often come home with less fish than is allowed. Somewhere along the way you figure out that success in fishing isn't measured in number of fish or pounds of fish, but in the challenges you overcame to catch them. Where a couple years ago you turned loose the little fish and kept the big ones, now you release the big ones and just keep a few small ones.

Somewhere along the way you figure out that angling isn't about catching fish, it's about having fun. You are no longer one of the 90%. When you have learned that hunting isn't really about pulling the trigger and killing, it's about knowing your quarry and his habits. When you pass up on that year old forked horn buck, and decide to wait for a trophy buck that has reached his prime and has already passed on his genes, congratulations, you have arrived! You have become one of the 10%.

⌘ ⌘ ⌘

DEATH IN THE WILDERNESS

March 2010

In October 2005, a 22 year old graduate student in Saskatchewan had the dubious distinction of being the first documented human wolf fatality in North America in about a hundred years. Last week, Candace Berner, a 32 year old special education teacher in Chignik Lake, Alaska was out jogging when she was attacked and killed by a pack of wolves. A couple years ago, Timothy Tredwell who had become notorious as "The Grizzly Man" was found in Katmai Alaska, by the bush pilot who had come to fly him out to civilization. Along with Treadwell's partially eaten body, officials also found the remains of his girlfriend as well. It isn't clear whether the couple had been eaten by one or two bears.

In addition to the two recent wolf kills, in the past few years, there have been over 30 fatal bear attacks in North America along with 5 documented mountain lion kills, and 5 deaths attributed to snake bite. Although the huge brown bears and grizzlies get all the publicity, actually, almost half the human deaths have been reliably attributed to black bears. Just this past July, a California woman out walking her dogs in the mountains east of Bakersfield, was attacked and seriously injured by a black bear. Experts believe that the recent California wildfires have driven bears into new areas in search of food.

In the southern U.S. there have been about a half dozen fatal alligator attacks in the past decade, while sharks have killed about a dozen people in the same time period. Golly gee! The woods must be teeming with danger what with so many folks being killed and all. Bull! With close to 500 million people in North America, your odds are about a million to one against being killed by a wild critter. Of course, there are dangers in the wild, but I'd venture that you're more likely to get killed in a drive by shooting or run over by a drunk driver. I once heard a cute vignette about how a city slicker remarked to the old wilderness guide, "Gosh, there things out there that can kill you!" to which the old timer replied, "If there ain't somthin out there that can kill you, it ain't a wilderness!"

While there are indeed things out in the wild that can kill you, a few simple precautions can greatly improve your odds. Keeping a clean camp is probably the simplest way to avoid bear trouble. Wash your dishes as soon as you've finished eating and store your food in bear proof containers or suspended high in a tree out of reach. Never take food into your tent or sleeping bag.

When camping, even when it's not hunting season, I carry a handgun to scare bears away with a warning shot between his legs. If absolutely necessary, you can dispatch a bear with a handgun. When I expressed reservations about the wisdom or effectiveness of shooting a bear with a handgun, an old time bear hunter said "Son, you just stick the gun in the bear's ear and pull the trigger. It works every time." I suspected the old boy was pulling my leg, until I found myself up close and personal with a very angry bear. Darned if he wasn't right!

Do I recommend carrying a big hog-leg strapped to your waist whenever you are out in the woods? Not unless you know how to use it, and feel comfortable carrying one. While back packing years ago with my young wife and my parents, I rounded a bend in the trail and surprised a large rattler who decided to come straight at me. Fortunately, I had my handgun readily reachable on my pack and a single shot killed him at a distance of 6 feet.

Although that particular snake was shot with a solid bullet, snakeshot in a handgun is incredibly effective, even if you're a lousy shot. You just instinctively draw and fire, and the snakes head vanishes. I use a revolver with snakeshot because it never jams. The first round is snakeshot and ensuing rounds are solid bullets. That way if I encounter a bear or boar, I can quickly rotate the cylinder past the shot cartridge and have a round suitable for dropping a large critter if necessary.

If you're uncomfortable with a gun, you can carry pepper spray for bear deterrence or two legged snakes. Other precautions include having a snake bite kit with you in the wild, and a cell phone or GPS locator with which to summon help. Probably the best safety precaution of all is to pay attention to your surroundings. Watch where you walk and you'll avoid a lot of trouble.

Another great safety feature is a dog. If you are along the stream and your family dog begins to growl while the hair stands up on the back of his neck, you may wish to unsnap the safety strap on your gun. I've had that happen before and the dog stood close to me and kept growling for almost a half hour. I never saw the critter and don't know if it was a lion, or a bear or even a whacko human, but that old dog earned his keep that day.

Don't let me scare you, statistically, you're far safer in the wild than almost anywhere else, just take a few simple precautions and your outdoor experience should be a great one.

⌘ ⌘ ⌘

THE GHOST OF MARCY'S MEADOW

July 1985

As we walked across the meadow toward the big split boulder on the far edge, my seven year old daughter, Julie, asked "Where's the plaque, Daddy?" I replied, "It's at the base of the big rock, Honey," and pointed to the boulder which had been split eons ago. A brass plaque proclaiming the place "Marcy's Meadow" had been set in mortar sheltered between the two granite halves. I couldn't help but think of the old hymn's opening lines "Rock of Ages, cleft for me. Let me hide myself in thee..."

My thoughts were interrupted by another question, "Is Marcy buried there, Daddy?" I explained that Marcy was buried in a cemetery in town, and Julie said, "Well is her ghost here, then?" I responded "I guess maybe it is Honey, but it's a friendly ghost."

Marcy had been more like family than simply a friend. Over almost 30 years our three families had camped together every summer – the Moyers, Hodges, and Neumans. In fact we grew so close we referred to ourselves as the MoHoNeu Tribe. We camped, fished, chased chipmunks and counted stars around the campfire. Whenever we squabbled as kids, whichever mother was closest, would cuff us, much like a mother bear with her cubs. We grew up together and went to each others graduations, bachelor parties, weddings, and baby showers. The MoHoNeu Tribe grew from three families to a dozen.

When I think of a vacation, I naturally think of going right back to the same place I have always gone for vacations, Hermit Valley at the top of Ebbetts Pass. Of course to most normal folks that would be pretty dull. I never get to Hawaii, haven't been to Paris, and probably will never cruise the Caribbean in a sailboat. Its pretty poor ammunition for chatter at cocktail parties, too. When others are talking about the magnificent view of the Alps, I really don't make much of an impression when I casually mention that the view is fantastic from Wolf Creek Pass.

Don't get me wrong, I like to travel as well as the next person. Heck, I chase rainbows in California, Browns in Pennsylvania, Cutthroats in Pyramid, and Smallmouth in the Potomac. Somehow, vacations seem as though they ought to be taken in familiar surroundings. My neighbor vacationed when he was a kid at a little creek west of Chico. He still goes there with his family and tells his kids tales of when he was catching frogs from the very rock his kids stood upon this year.

I like the memories that become associated with the happy times of vacation. There were no funerals, no drugs, nor political assassinations. Instead there are memories of cranking the ice cream freezer until your arm ached, and how good that ice cream tasted when you finally got to eat it; getting caught in a summer thunderstorm, and of roasting fresh trout over a streamside fire. Every time I visit the outhouse, I think of the great outhouse fire.

Whenever I see Julie playing in the creek, I think of the dam we built each summer and how it washed out every spring and we had to build it over again. Driving around Deadmans Curve, I remember the time the steering wheel came off the jeep!

In the evenings, we often take a walk down the back trail to see if we can spot a browsing deer. I'm sure it must have been caused by too much wine at happy hour, but as I walked at dusk, into the edge of Marcy's Meadow, I could have sworn I saw a woman in jeans and a plaid blouse bending down to pick up an arrowhead. I blinked and looked again, but she was gone. Yep, too much wine. There probably aren't any ghosts out there, but if there are, I'll bet they're friendly ones.

⌘ ⌘ ⌘

18816191R00165

Made in the USA
Charleston, SC
22 April 2013